When You Are the Partner of a Rape or Incest Survivor

A Workbook for You

Robert Barry Levine

Resource Publications, Inc.
San Jose, California

Editorial director: Kenneth Guentert
Managing editor: Elizabeth J. Asborno
Copyeditor: Leila T. Bulling

Resource Publications, Inc.
160 E. Virginia Street #290
San Jose, CA 95112-5876

ISBN 0-89390-329-9

Printed in the United States of America

00 99 98 97 96 | 5 4 3 2

Contents

Dedication

For approximately the last six years, I have been fortunate enough to be a counselor at The Valley Trauma Center in Northridge, California. This is where my path began, and I dedicate this workbook to each and every client I have worked with.

I am grateful to the survivors for their trust in the Center and in me. I recognize their honesty, courage, and devotion to their healing. I also commend the courage of the partners who attended the support groups. They, too, chose to take a path of education and exploration into many feelings and emotions.

I affectionately remember the closeness and specialness attached to each of my clients and support groups.

Acknowledgments

Special thanks to Johanna Gallers. Through your beliefs and dedication, the Valley Trauma Center was able to get its start. It is your faith and confidence in me that prompted me to begin this project.

To my fellow counselors at the center who were my co-facilitators: Gretchen Lampert, Mary Ellen Thompson, Elise Cohen, Carole Gogan, Lisa Melton, and Kirstin Friant. Your hard work and dedication to the groups were vital to their success.

To the members of my thesis committee: Luis Rubalcava, PhD, Charles Hanson, PhD, and Christine Kaye Campbell, PhD. You each gave me inspiration and support.

To Laurie B. for giving me the strength to trust in myself and continue my work in this area even when it got close to home. Though our paths may not cross now, you will always be special.

To my parents, brother, and sister-in-law: you have been a source of unconditional love and support.

Thank you, John Hatcher. Your computer and printing assistance were tremendous helps in the completion of this project.

Special thanks to the people at Resource Publications, Inc., for their efforts in the publication of this book.

Introduction

"Walking on Eggshells"

For the past several years I have worked as a counselor at a trauma center. The clientele were survivors of rape, incest, and molestation. Through the center, various types of counseling services were offered to the clients, e.g., individual therapy, survivor support groups, crisis counseling, and couples therapy.

Though counseling was also available to survivors' family members, a support group was not available for their partners. During my internship at the center, it became apparent that such a counseling service could benefit both partners and survivors. The couples themselves communicated thoughts and feelings on how a partners support group would help them.

The Survivors

The survivors expressed an interest in a partners support group in the hope that it would help their mates better understand what survivors go through. Incest survivors were concerned that their mates didn't fully understand the long-term impact that childhood sexual abuse has. Did partners really understand the family dynamics involved?

What about all the feelings the survivors were forced to repress?

Many incest survivors wanted their partners to understand why keeping the abuse a secret had become important—sharing the story would cause disruption and chaos in the family, and the survivors would be blamed for tearing the family apart.

Survivors also wanted their partners to realize how critical creating boundaries of safety is. These boundaries help survivors regain a sense of control in their lives. Setting boundaries is not about dominating and controlling relationships; rather, setting boundaries is about empowering themselves—adapting new ways of coping and reclaiming their self-esteem.

Some survivors expressed concern that their partners didn't realize that healing takes time. Victims of incest were usually forced into a world of darkness and isolation wherein feelings were not validated. Victims were left with a sense of helplessness and hopelessness, believing their pain would endure forever. This sensation tends to surface again and again on the road to healing.

Rape survivors wished their mates would better understand the impact a sexual assault has on the survivor's sense of self. Victims of rape are often left with self-blame and the belief that somehow the rape was their fault.

Whether victims of date rape, acquaintance rape, marital rape, or stranger rape, survivors feel shame and bewilderment. "What did I do to deserve this?" This false belief doesn't fade away easily and leaves a scar that lasts a lifetime. When survivors finally accept the reality that the rape wasn't their fault, compassion and validation from the partners is critical reinforcement.

Many survivors wanted their mates to understand how sexual assaults and molestations have long-term impact on the ability to trust others. Whether the violation is a broken boundary by a parent or society's revictimization during a rape trial, the impact can be felt years down the road. Many survivors wonder if they can ever trust again—or whether they will have to isolate themselves from their family and the outside world.

The Partners

What about the partners' concerns? What were they looking for? Many partners were interested in a support group for several reasons. One primary reason was their desire to learn all the "right" things to say and do because they believed some of their behaviors and statements were revictimizing their mates. They wanted to be perfect companions, but they believed they couldn't say or do anything right. They were walking on eggshells.

This belief by the partners led them to blame themselves any time the survivors felt rage or depression, acted withdrawn, or experienced a flashback. Partners became frantic and subsequently overcompensated when interacting with the survivors on physical and emotional levels. Once stuck in this cycle, both partners and survivors built up feelings of resentment as frustration increased.

Partners also wanted to know how to handle the anger their mates exhibited. Was there a better way to manage all this displaced anger? Was this anger directed at them somehow justifiable because of the abuse the survivors encountered?

Partners had additional concerns about the sexual relationship: How long does it usually take for survivors to become comfortable enough to resume a sexual relationship? Were the partners wrong for wanting this part of the relationship to continue? What about spontaneity in the partners' desire to be sexually intimate—would that revictimize the survivors or trigger a flashback?

Partners expressed loss in other areas of their intimate relationships, such as emotional connectedness. Could that be rekindled, or would the survivors be too afraid and angry to let down their guard? Did the partners have to stay emotionally distanced to allow the survivors to heal?

Coupled with their regard for the survivors, partners were interested in dealing with their own needs and feelings. Were they entitled to have any (not to mention express them)? For instance, would it be okay for partners of incest survivors to express their rage at the perpetrator(s)? Could they tell the survivors how much they hated the family member who did this? Could partners of rape survivors openly express their anger toward the rapist, or would the survivors become concerned that the partners' rage would go out of control?

Along with anger, most partners were feeling loss but didn't know if they could show it for fear of overwhelming the survivors. They believed they had to hide their own grief because they were not the ones victimized.

With all these questions and concerns, partners wondered if they would actually get support from a group. Could counseling help them find the answers? Surprisingly (to many partners), a significant result of the group experience was the normalizing effect it had on its members. By attending a safe and therapeutic setting where other partners were expressing similar types of feelings, the partners realized they weren't alone. They no longer had to feel isolated in their concerns.

The support group helped the partners realize that they themselves had a process to go through. Their course would involve actions and reactions to the survivors, to the perpetrators, and to themselves. In time, they would learn to stop walking on eggshells.

This support group process for the partners led me to develop this workbook. It can be used by you on an individual basis or in a group setting with other partners. The exercises, however, work best when they can be explored and dealt with in a therapeutic setting.

At the end of some chapters, you will find narratives from other partners. These partners decided to attend support groups and began their own journeys into under-standing "partnership." Some of them chose to share por-tions of their journey with you.

Some Words of Caution

This workbook was designed to assist partners of survi-vors in their quest to maintain healthy relationships. The chapters were designed as introductions into each topic, supplying the reader with some general education and, where applicable, techniques and exercises to utilize. *At no time* is it recommended to force upon partners or survivors any of the material or exercises in this workbook.

This publication is not a cure-all and some parts con-tained within may or may not be suitable for all who read it. I offer these materials only as suggested guidelines. The exercises work best when you and your mate are in or have recently been in therapy (individual, group, or couples).

For further information and more specific details, please see the referrals, recommendations for further reading, and supportive organizations compiled in the chapter entitled "Resources."

Definitions of Terms

Specific terms in this text are those utilized in my work with survivors and partners. Definitions differ from state to state as do statutes of limitation for prosecution. (Note: If survivors choose to prosecute a perpetrator or perpetrators, I suggest contacting an attorney or researching the state law in which the victimization took place.)

Rape: Rape is the carnal knowledge of a female forcibly and against her will. Assaults or attempts to commit rape by force or threat of force are also included (defined by the Federal Bureau of

Investigation and as published in the Uniform Crime Reporting Program). As noted in my work, rape survivors include those victims of marital, date, and acquaintance rape as well as survivors of attempted rape. Rape includes any sexual act a person is forced to submit to.

Child Sexual Molestation or Abuse: Child sexual molestation or abuse is contact or interaction between a child and an adult when the child is being used for the sexual stimulation of the perpetrator or another person. Sexual abuse may also be committed by a person under the age of eighteen when that person is either significantly older than the victim or when the perpetrator is in a position of power or control over another child (defined by the National Center on Child Abuse and Neglect [NCCAN]).

Incest: Incest is the sexual molestation of a child by a blood relative or any adult in a position of authority and trust over that child, e.g., father, mother, step-parent, foster-parent, grandparent, legal guardian.

Partner: The partner is the significant other of the survivor. A partner can be either a spouse, fiancee, "steady," or lover. In essence, the partner is an individual involved in an intimate, monogamous relationship with the survivor. A partner does not have to be male or female; the relationship may be heterosexual, gay, or lesbian.

Survivor: The survivor is the individual who has been incested, sexually molested or abused, or raped (including attempted rape) as a minor and/or as an adult. A survivor does not have to be a particular gender.

Statistics on Sexual Assault against Adults and Children

- An estimated one in four girls and one in seven boys are sexually abused by the time they reach age eighteen.[1]

- In 1985, a poll conducted throughout the United States found that twenty-seven percent of all women and sixteen percent of all men reported being molested as children.[2]

- The FBI estimated that in the year 1993 there were 104,806 forcible rapes in the United States alone.[3]

- The U.S. Senate reported in June 1990 that a woman is raped every six minutes and that she is ten times more likely to be raped than to die in a car crash.[4]

- The U.S. Senate reported that serious crimes against women were rising nearly four times as fast as the total crime rate for the past decade.[5]

- Each year more than one million women seek medical assistance for injuries caused by battering.[6]

- Three out of four women will be victims of at least one violent crime during their lifetimes.[7]

---

[1] Laura Davis, *Allies in Healing: When the Person You Love Was Sexually Abused As a Child* (New York: Harper Perennial, 1991), 1.

[2] *Los Angeles Times Poll*, 1985.

[3] Federal Bureau of Investigation, *Crime Reports in the United States 1993* (Washington, DC: U.S. Government Printing Office, 1993).

[4] Linda Schmittroth, ed., *Statistical Record of Women Worldwide* (Detroit, Michigan: Gale Research, Inc., 1991), 75.

[5] Ibid.

[6] Ibid.

[7] Ibid.

One

Telling Your Story

One of the most important things that a family member, friend, or therapist can suggest to survivors is to have them tell their story. All too often, survivors believe that keeping the attack a secret is their duty. Whether they are children who were sexually molested or adults who were raped, many survivors believe keeping their victimization a secret is best.

In keeping this secret, survivors tend to lock away important and often repressed feelings such as sadness, hurt, and anger. These are only a few of the key emotions that must come to the surface for exploration. With key feelings remaining hidden, survivors experience a sense of shame, worthlessness, helplessness and the belief that somehow they were to blame.

The healing process helps teach survivors that they are survivors because of their strengths and not their weaknesses. By sharing the story of how they were violated and by exploring locked-away emotions, they can begin to heal. This sharing and exploration are only part of the process and work that lie ahead for the survivor.

How does this affect you, the partner? What is your story? Just like the survivor, you too may feel that you must keep your pain, suffering, and anger a secret. You may even think that you have no right to bring up your own "stuff." You might think that your needs aren't as important, and so you focus on taking care of the survivor.

The fact remains, however, that you must have a place to tell your story, a place to go where you can feel safe enough to disclose pent-up emotions and have them validated. Whether you choose to attend a support group or individual therapy, to share your story with a best friend, or any combination of these, you need a place to vent.

This doesn't mean that you can't share your feelings and needs at home with the survivor. It means that you, like the survivor, need a source of support outside your home, a place where it is okay to take some time and to be there for yourself.

Similar to the survivor's, your story may remain untold for several possible reasons. If you are a male partner, one reason for your silence may be the old societal belief that as a man you must remain the stronghold, the caretaker of the home and all its inhabitants. You can't hold down the fort when you have to bother dealing with your emotional side. And let's not forget the myth that says men don't know how to get in touch with their emotions, except maybe anger.

If you are a female partner, you may choose not to tell your story for fear of being labeled "over-emotional." Perhaps you are afraid of being called a "nag" if you try to discuss the survivor's displaced anger.

Regardless of your gender, one of the most common reasons that you will not want to share your story is because you feel guilty. This guilt comes from the tendency to undermine your own hurt and pain (something that survivors are known to do as well).

Partners often believe that their needs are less important than those of survivors because of all that the survivors have been through. As a partner, you seem to forget what you are going through in an effort to support your mate.

You may consider yourself only after you consider what is best for the survivor.

Reluctance to share your story can also come from your fear of triggering the survivor into an angry outburst, of which you would probably become the target. With this belief, you place the responsibility of how the survivor feels and reacts squarely on your own shoulders. Your existence becomes only a reaction to how you perceive the survivor will act. Talk about walking on eggshells!

And what if you are a parent, uncle or aunt, grandparent, or just someone who comes in close contact with kids—will there be additional concerns for you? Survivors (primarily those who were sexually abused as children) who are parents will often express additional fears and concerns about the safety of their children or other children with whom they are in contact. They seem to bear a heightened sense of fear and concern.

This situation plays a role in your life, too. You may find that your actions and behaviors around children are cautiously monitored by the survivor and even yourself. Both the close examination by your mate and yourself can cause additional tension and stress in your relationship.

You may think that your desire and subsequent display of affection toward children borders on inappropriate conduct. Eventually, you begin to monitor more closely your interactions with children, e.g., taking a bath with your baby, bouncing a child on your knee, changing the baby's diaper, hugging the children. Behaviors that are routine and of a second nature may cause you to think twice as you develop a sense of paranoia.

If you are re-evaluating your display of affection toward children, look at your motivation. Taking a bath with your baby or bouncing a child on your knee for the enjoyment of sharing a tender moment is far different than touching and fondling a child for sexual pleasure and control. Use your sensitivity and awareness of child molestation as an aid to help those children you think have been abused and not to drive yourself crazy.

For more guidance about caring touches with children, please refer to the chapter entitled "Resources." Under the sub-heading of Children's Books on Abuse, you will find some excellent reading materials to inform yourself about the area of child sexual abuse.

In general, you may not have an easy time expressing your needs and wants in the relationship once the survivor has started to work on her/his healing. You may not feel ready to tell your story. It might be important to consider taking a look at the first step in understanding what it means to be a partner.

Take a moment now to think of some reason(s) why you haven't shared your feelings and needs with your mate. After a few minutes, jot down your reasons here:

1. _____
   _____

2. _____
   _____

3. _____
   _____

4. _____
   _____

5. _____
   _____

Once you have made the conscious decision to accept your feelings, needs, and desires, you must then learn constructive ways to express them. This work can and will be as difficult as it is rewarding. Some of the partners I have worked with over the last couple of years have shared that this work was only the beginning for them. They found that exploring their present relationships and the issues that arose for them was a gateway into looking at other areas in their past and present.

The "What Are Your Needs?" Exercise

The following exercise will help you get a better understanding of how many needs you might be stuffing or keeping inside. You may choose to repeat this exercise at different times during your work as a partner.

You might find that some of your needs have been satisfied while new ones have come up. There is no right or wrong way of doing this exercise. Its value lies only in that it opens you up to what your needs are in the relationship.

Through your continued work as a partner, you will begin to learn which needs can be satisfied by the survivor, yourself, others, or a combination. You may learn which of your needs are unrealistic expectations and which ones are within reason. You can also separate those needs that were recurrent themes in your former relationship(s) from those that only arise in this relationship.

EXERCISE: THE "WHAT ARE YOUR NEEDS?" LIST

List the needs, feelings, and thoughts that you are presently "stuffing" or think you are unable to express in this relationship.

1. _____

2. _____

3. _____

4. _____

5. _____

6. _____

7. _____

8. _____

9. _____

10._____

Carefully examine the list you just created and choose two or three of the most important items to write about in the next exercise.

WRITING EXERCISE: "WHAT ARE YOUR NEEDS?"

In the previous exercise, you chose two or three items from your list to write about. Include in the writing what it has been like to withhold these needs and feelings. Take into account whether or not these items on your list have come up in your past relationship(s). If they have, write about how you dealt with them at that time and how you intend to cope with them now.

When you have completed the writing exercise, read it aloud to yourself. Take note of how you feel while reading it. Do you find yourself becoming angry? Do you feel sad? Are you feeling disappointed with how you have been handling the situation? Are you pleased with how you have reacted?

After you have completed the exercise, I encourage you to share the results with your counselor, therapist, and/or support group for further exploration and awareness.

_____

_____

_____

_____

_____

_____

_____

_____

WRITING EXERCISE: "WHAT ARE YOUR NEEDS?"
(*continued*)

_____

_____

_____

_____

_____

_____

_____

_____

_____

_____

_____

_____

_____

_____

WRITING EXERCISE: "WHAT ARE YOUR NEEDS?"
(*continued*)

_____

_____

_____

_____

_____

_____

_____

_____

_____

_____

_____

_____

_____

Ed's Story

Reactions to being a partner.

When I first learned about my wife being a survivor, I was confused. I didn't know what to think. I didn't know how to react. I tried to think how she felt about it. She was so cool that I tended to downplay it because she seemed to be handling it so well. I had no idea, at that time, that she wasn't handling it very well. I was a little bewildered and stunned by the stories she was telling, but because she didn't react to the stories, it was like she was telling someone else's stories.

The emotional ups and downs between good times was really dramatic. I've never been exposed to what I call "inappropriate anger," anger about the smallest things. Where I put something could trigger a really big emotional outburst. That was something I didn't understand and that was going on from almost the beginning: emotional outbursts.

I would try not to antagonize her. I would walk on egg shells around her, figuring that maybe I upset her somehow. To me it was having to be too careful around someone you are supposed to be intimate with and in love with. I objected to it. It was driving a wedge in our relationship to the point where I started thinking I didn't want to be in the relationship.

I didn't have any real strong emotions toward the perpetrator, but from what I understood happened, a lot of hate could have come out. Right now I'm hearing some awful stories that I can't imagine anybody doing to anybody. He's an evil person.

I mean, really truly an evil person and I think someone else out there is probably getting hurt right now by the same person. I really believe that. I don't think he should be free.

Your needs, the survivor's needs.

Well, I didn't think my needs were getting met. I thought we were living a life of dealing with her emotions, her anger, her uneven temperament. When my wife was happy, then I could be happy. Instead of dealing with my own problems, I was always reacting to hers.

I think what I missed was some of the warmness that I wanted from her. Our relationship became usually more mechanical. It was all sweet or all angry; there was no genuine warmness and I felt cheated. When I started dealing with her anger, I really felt cheated and it got to the point where I wanted out because it wasn't satisfying for me.

What was missing for me was the warm, playful person I wanted to be around. She was too cool, happy, and angry in varying degrees. She was not even. It felt difficult to be close to her and I wanted to be close to someone. That's my style; that's my nature. I need to be close to someone. I need to be able to be vulnerable in front of somebody. I need to trust somebody, and with her emotions being unpredictable I didn't feel like I could get that close.

Her needs? She definitely needed understanding and as I learned more and more, she needed to feel that she was not to blame. She had grown up and lived with blame for a long, long time, for the last twenty years.

I think that is one of the reasons why she didn't talk about it in more depth. She was afraid someone would blame her for her part in it, when in reality she was the victim.

I made some comments during that time such as, "How could that go on for eight years? How could that go on after you were married (the first time)?" She would be very angry and turn off because she thought it was a blaming statement. Maybe it was, but to me it was bewilderment.

She needed to be told it wasn't her fault because it wasn't. That was what I had to get through. Realizing it wasn't her fault even though it went on for a long period of time. I used to think, why didn't she run away? Why would anyone stay if she were being treated that way? It would be better to live on the street than to live in those conditions. Having not gone through that myself and having lived in a pretty normal family, I couldn't understand the feelings that would go on, or the situation.

Sam's Story

Hearing about incest for the first time.

It's been about two years since my wife discovered this and it's a very difficult time for both of us trying to cope together. At first it was very chaotic and of course I had very little understanding until I got into some of the literature about the healing process. Once that started, I had a better understanding of what was going on. Over the two years I'd say the relationship is still fairly difficult.

I thought it was unbelievably awful that she went through this. It was a little hard for me to relate because I came from a family that was very unlike hers; it was almost dull by comparison. There was very little going on, in fact there wasn't any kind of abuse—sexual, verbal, or physical—in my family.

It was very shocking to me and I had never known anyone who ever admitted that they had been through this. It was a shock and I felt very bad for her. I felt awful about these people. I found it hard to believe that these people had done this. I definitely believed her; she wouldn't say it unless she really, really knew it to be true.

My needs.

I needed companionship, intimacy, someone that was interested in some of things I was interested in and to just laugh a little bit. A sense of humor has always been a very important thing to me, the ability to smile at life. That really disappeared immediately, all of that. I felt really lonely in a way and kind of not in touch at all.

Our sexual relationship took a turn for the worse from my point of view. We had a couple different periods of celibacy in the first year and she would often have flashbacks during sexual activity. It was very difficult and still is very difficult.

In my opinion our sex life is still quite sub-standard in frequency and in experience. It still isn't back to what I would like and I don't know when it will be, if ever. I'm very disappointed. I feel like I'm missing out on some of the good things in life.

I work awfully hard and I just feel like I'm not living as full a life as I could. I know that it isn't easy for her going through this—I'm aware of that—but I'm getting a little discouraged about it after two years. I just don't know if it's ever going to improve and that is disappointing, discouraging, and makes me quite unhappy.

I really enjoy my job and the people I work with, so I've thrown myself into that. I talk to my friends a lot. I try and do my best at that. I get my entertainment, my laughter, and my feelings of belonging from my work and my children—a very, very important source.

My daughter and I are close and we have a very good relationship. She has the same sense of humor and we laugh a lot. We talk a lot and I help with her homework a great deal. So, I've thrown myself into the children and my work and try to meet my needs that way as much as I can.

Bill's Story

Finding out you are a partner.

For a great many years of our relationship we had no idea that my wife had been incested. As she discovered what had occurred in her past, it changed our relationship significantly. I guess I've experienced a little bit of anger, having to deal with this situation that I didn't know about when we got married.

I think the first thing that strikes me is she will be an incest survivor for the rest of her life. I do not expect things to go back to the way they were before. It's just something I accept now. I have to be sensitive to her situation.

She started becoming more fearful of intimate contact, physical contact. She was more emotionally sensitized to certain actions or ways of being. I was another one of those men. She became angry and didn't want to have sexual relations.

There were many, many months that went by without us making love at all. I was getting a little frustrated with all this and not understanding what was going on. It happened so long ago; what did it have to do with our marriage? I love her and I would never force myself on her, so why was she taking this out on me?

I had to change to a certain degree within myself if I wanted to stay in this relationship. It forced me to find out what was really going on with her and how I could make my life and our relationship fulfilling for myself, as well as for her.

Now she knows I have a better understanding of what is going on with her. We've talked about it many times and so she is more willing to be honest with me, like, "Hey, I'm feeling very sensitive today; please be very careful with me." So, we are having more honest communication, which really helps both of us from going underground with our feelings.

Jack's Story

In the beginning.

She was a survivor of an attempted rape and I was involved from just about five minutes after the attack. Initially, I was very concerned for her physical well-being, as she was pretty bruised and battered. Secondly, I was concerned for her mental well-being. Then, the third point would be the impact it would have on our marriage as a whole. Maybe, somewhat selfishly, I was also thinking about our sexual relations too. Everything I've read and heard said survivors become totally different people. That was kind of what was running through my head.

We've gone through ups and downs, plus we had other outside issues that entered into it. It was definitely rocky and there were times when I was ready to throw my hands up and say "That's it." And, you know, quite honestly I still have those moments, but they're not anywhere near as strong as they were a year and a half ago, even six months ago.

I guess the way it's affected us is initially I became very aware of survivors. She went through her own counseling and her own support group. She shared with me everything that went on in her group and I shared everything with her that went on in my group. We both became knowledgeable, I of her feelings and her of mine. During that process our communication with each other became stronger.

Two

Building Your Support Network

- Can you really get help from a support group?
- Are there needs that you can have validated by a group of other partners?
- Do partners have the right to express their feelings?
- Will you as a partner ever feel upset, frustrated, sad, aggravated, hurt, angry, helpless, and hopeless?

The answer to each and every question above is *yes!* You, too, have been victimized. Though you may not have been a direct victim of the violation, you are indeed affected on an emotional and psychological level.

Just like the survivor, you will be forced to deal with many emotions, some of which you may not feel comfortable expressing. You might easily express certain emotions but the survivor might not validate them because s/he is experiencing emotional conflict at that time. Regardless, you will feel drained periodically.

For example, take the feeling of anger. This emotion may be difficult for you to share because of the way you were raised and because of your fears surrounding its expression. Combine those fears with the thought of scaring the survivor with your rage, and chances are good that you will suppress the anger until you reach your breaking point.

Many of the emotions you feel along with anger, such as sadness, loneliness, and helplessness, can also be difficult for you to express to the survivor for fear that they won't get validated. You may find yourself struggling to suppress many of the same emotions that survivors suppress. The reason(s) for such suppression of feelings may even be the same for each of you in that you feel vulnerable in letting your guard down; you feel uneasy that your mate won't show regard for what you have laid out on the table.

With all the different emotions that come into play with being a partner (anger, sadness, hurt, guilt, loneliness, frustration, helplessness, fear, aggravation, and so forth), the need for support outside the home is a critical issue in preventing you from feeling resentful.

One thing partners support groups teach is the importance of learning how to take care of yourself. You must learn how to examine your needs and to subsequently express what you are feeling.

It is rather difficult to take care of and/or give support to someone else before taking care of yourself. You might put yourself in a position of second best as you attempt to support the survivor. The result is that your needs don't get met and, after a period of time, you may find yourself harboring resentment toward your mate.

Perhaps you even feel guilty or responsible for having not protected your mate (primarily in cases of rape). You may think that you let your mate down, and now you will do everything in your power to ensure that this will never happen again. This usually starts with your attempts to accommodate the survivor's every need. You will actually come to believe it is within your power to *make* the survivor *feel* safe.

If you are a partner of an incest survivor, you may not have feelings of guilt because the molestation occurred prior to your relationship. However, you may feel the same need and responsibility to make certain that the survivor feels safe. If the perpetrator was a family member, you may try to shield the survivor from any type of contact with that family member.

Holidays, funerals, and special occasions like birthdays, weddings, anniversaries, and graduations are times when family members gather together. During these periods you may find yourself being overprotective of your mate. You rationalize that it is your responsibility to decide which family members are appropriate for the survivor to see or come in contact with. Knowingly or not, you take on the role of an overprotective parent.

I have found the support group to be one of the best ways for partners to get in touch with many thoughts and feelings regarding what happened to the survivors and to themselves. The group provides you with a chance to explore and open up. As you and the group evolve, you will have opportunities to get in touch with issues and emotions lying beneath those you express.

Support doesn't have to come only from the support group. Individual therapy is another great way to get in touch with your feelings and the underlying issues. In fact, individual therapy affords you the opportunity to be completely selfish as you explore how other areas may intertwine in your relationship with your mate.

Just like the survivor, your support network can include close friends. Most of the partners in my groups have stated how they had one or two good friends whom they could lean on. Whether the friends were local or distant, reached by phone or through a visit, there were other people to listen to their stories.

Family members can also be an important part of your support network. You may confide in parents, siblings, cousins, or an aunt and uncle. Some members also choose to accept support from other groups like Alcoholics Anonymous, Adult Children of Alcoholics, religious organizations, and so forth. The important thing is that you don't have to face your ordeal alone.

Don't forget the survivor as part of your support network. Right now, your mate may not seem a practical or even attainable part of your network. You might think, "The survivor has her/his hands full dealing with the healing process, so how can s/he have time to give me support?" On the contrary, during the healing process, there are times when the survivor would like nothing better than to take time out from her/his work and give you some support. Just like you, the survivor has a need to play caretaker, too. S/he may want to take some time to validate your feelings and acknowledge your hard work in the relationship during a time of crisis. Remember, your relationship has to be a two-way street: give and take.

EXERCISE: BUILDING YOUR SUPPORT NETWORK

See what kind of a list you can put together in establishing your own support network. List as many different resources as you can. For some possible suggestions, include the following: friends, family members, spouse, therapist, organizations, groups, or a clergyman.

Name _____ Phone _____
How This Person Will Support Me

_____

_____

_____

Name _____ Phone _____
How This Person Will Support Me

_____

_____

_____

Name _____ Phone _____
How This Person Will Support Me

_____

_____

_____

Name _____ Phone _____
How This Person Will Support Me

_____

_____

_____

EXERCISE: BUILDING YOUR SUPPORT NETWORK
(*continued*)

Name _____ Phone _____
How This Person Will Support Me

_____

_____

_____

Name _____ Phone _____
How This Person Will Support Me

_____

_____

_____

Name _____ Phone _____
How This Person Will Support Me

_____

_____

_____

Name _____ Phone _____
How This Person Will Support Me

_____

_____

_____

Name _____ Phone _____
How This Person Will Support Me

_____

_____

_____

Jack's Story

Striking a balance.

The tendency is, since she's gone through so much, you need to take care of her, but you need to take care of yourself, too. I know for the first six months to a year I was looking to get into a support group. My wife was constantly saying, "Have you looked here, have you looked there?" I really didn't actively look. I didn't think I needed it. I thought I could handle it.

I didn't have a clue what was going on in her head and didn't have a clue what was going on in my head until I got into the group. I can honestly say that the group saved our marriage. Not having gone through it, there's no way I could have understood what was going on. The need to talk about it and understand what's going on is imperative.

The other part is time. Take time; you can't rush things. Everyone heals in different ways over different periods of time. I think it depends on the individual and where he is, mentally and psychologically, to determine how much time it takes to heal. I looked at this as short term—in six months everything will be fine. I kept saying to her, "When are you going to stop doing this? When are you going to stop yelling at the television, at commercials? When are you going to stop reading an article in the paper and ripping it up to feel better?"

I think you can't put artificial time limits on it. You have to realize that everyone has his own recovery period and you can't set the time limits. You need to be patient. You have to do what's right for you, the relationship, and the survivor, but don't rush anything. Be patient!

Bill's Story

Coping

I don't have a real good background on how to deal with anger. My parents never expressed a lot of anger in our household. In fact, I never saw them yell at one another the whole time growing up. So, I felt kind of at a loss on how to deal with my anger and my feelings that this was unfair.

I started working harder and began ignoring her, not purposely, but throwing myself into things that took up just about all of my time. I had no real energy left for her. I rationalized that I was working hard, trying to support my family, bringing in some money, and creating a better life for ourselves. However, it wasn't necessarily creating a better life for us emotionally or mentally.

The most difficult thing in being a partner is being helpless—not being able to change what happened. If I can do something to make a change or make things work better, it would be easier than doing nothing. Also, not getting my own needs met and knowing that I cannot expect them to get met in a certain manner was difficult. It's been a long-term process to getting some of my needs met. Not out of expectations or demands, but by slowly working through it.

I don't think I could have ever made it or continued in my relationship without the help of the support group. Without the information on what an incest survivor goes through, I don't think our marriage would have lasted. What I valued most was being able to hear the similarities of what other men went through, getting their support, and being able to voice my feelings.

By going through the sessions here at the center, I have become more honest with my feelings. When I'm feeling angry about something, I express it truly, honestly, and immediately instead of holding on to it. There were times when I had some really strong feelings. It would have seemed inappropriate to communicate them to my wife, but I had a place to communicate them: the support group. People would listen to me and be honest in their responses to my feelings.

Three

Your Role in the Healing Process

Some research has shown that the survivor's healing process can be aided by a support network. This may include the therapist, partner, family members, or close friends. The survivor will know best which person or persons will be most understanding and supportive to her/his healing.

If you are reading this book, then it is highly probable that you are one of those people whom the survivor has included in her/his network. You can have a negative or positive effect on the survivor's healing process. Regardless of your intentions and motives, some of your actions, behaviors, and statements will have a negative impact, the brunt of which can be long lasting.

There are no guarantees on how to have a positive impact on the survivor's healing process all the time. This text serves only as an aid in your efforts to minimize the potential negative effects you can create.

As the partner, it is not your responsibility to make sure that the survivor begins the healing process or to determine the rate at which the process will go. Control of when to attend support groups with other survivors, the beginning and ending of individual therapy, and the decision to work on short- and long-term therapeutic issues belong to the survivor.

Your support for the survivor is best displayed when you respect her/his decision about how s/he chooses to heal—with the exception of harm to self or others. One of the biggest pitfalls that you can fall into is challenging a decision the survivor makes regarding her/his own therapy.

The following questions are examples of challenging:

- Did you ask the therapist how much longer this stuff will take?

- So, what happened in tonight's session?

- Do you really want to continue your therapy when all you do is get angry anyway?

- Are you sure therapy is helping you? It seems to make you cry a lot lately.

- Are you feeling better yet?

- So, what do you really do in one of those support groups anyway—sit around and talk about how awful we partners are?

- Why are you going to therapy now if this happened when you were a child?

- How come you can talk to the therapist about this stuff, but you won't talk to me about it?

- What are some of the other survivors' stories like?

When you challenge the survivor by asking questions like these, you re-victimize the survivor and contribute to her/his sense of vulnerability. Subsequently, you reinforce the belief that s/he has little to no competence in expressing emotions freely. When you ask these challenging questions, your concern isn't about the survivor's well-being but about your own uneasiness surrounding the abuse. Your frustration and hurt cause you to push the survivor along.

In choosing to support your mate's process of healing, you may sometimes be used as a sounding board. This role is not one partners usually volunteer for but often get picked for anyway. In this role, you wind up taking the brunt of displaced anger and pent-up rage. It isn't easy being the target of someone else's rage and anger when all you did was walk in the door. Sometimes it might seem that the survivor is looking for a fight.

The key to being an effective sounding board is to avoid becoming defensive and to allow the survivor a safe place to vent her/his feelings. There will be times when you just don't want to hear anymore, and that's okay. You must also take care of yourself. Strike a balance between giving the survivor room to vent and allowing yourself room to breathe.

It isn't okay for the survivor to take out the unfairness of the victimization on you. Having been abused isn't a green light for the survivor to abuse others verbally, emotionally, or physically. You may need to remind the survivor of this when s/he inappropriately takes out on you the anger s/he feels toward her/his perpetrator.

You have the right to protect yourself from abuse without abusing the survivor. This might seem like an impossible challenge, but neither person needs to escalate an already hot situation. Ways to specifically deal with anger are in the chapter entitled "Anger."

As a partner, you may also become a part-time caretaker. The survivor's need for self-empowerment is important; however, there will be times when the survivor needs to be that "little child" again. The survivor might need to know that there is at least one person in her/his life whom s/he can trust, lean on, and feel safe with. During these times, the survivor will want to rely on your strength. Do this by giving helpful suggestions if asked, having an open ear, or just being there when s/he asks for comfort.

Another way you can support the survivor's healing process is to let her/him know it wasn't her/his fault. The survivor may already believe that s/he was to blame, that s/he did something wrong, and/or that s/he did something to deserve the victimization. As a key person in the survivor's life, there is nobody better than you to help reinforce that s/he did nothing wrong. Let her/him know that s/he doesn't have to blame her/himself for what happened.

The survivor usually carries self-blame from the moment s/he has been victimized to the time s/he starts the process of healing. Your reinforcement in this area can certainly assist the survivor in coming to the realization that s/he was the victim and not the guilty party.

Do not to pass judgment on how the survivor handled her/his earlier victimization. The survivor might already feel ashamed of the experience, and inferences by you regarding her/his coping strategies will only further assault the survivor's sense of low self-worth.

Support also comes in the form of respecting the survivor's need for setting and maintaining boundaries, some of which directly affect your relationship, including its intimacy. Survivors of rape, incest, or molestation experience the violation of boundaries. This is partly why survivors are called "victims." Perpetrators take control and force them into situations in which they feel helpless and hopeless over the outcome of their abuse.

As the survivor makes the decision to heal, s/he will gain control in her/his life by setting certain boundaries. In this way, the survivor exhibits that s/he can take care of her/himself. Setting boundaries also represents the survivor's need for not only physical space but also emotional and psychological space. The survivor's decision to set a boundary doesn't always have to be futile. Your support shows the survivor that some people will respect another person's space.

Be supportive and openly acknowledge the survivor's gains in her/his healing. If you have witnessed a change in the actions, behaviors, or responses that the survivor has been working on, bring it to her/his attention. Let the survivor know that you recognize her/his hard work and dedication. Be honest and sincere in your disclosure; don't force it and don't be superficial. Phony acknowledgment minimizes your ability as a couple to work on healthy communication.

EXERCISE: YOUR ROLE IN THE HEALING PROCESS

List ways you can help support the survivor, either with actions or words. When you complete this exercise, you may want to share it with your mate.

1. _____
   _____
   _____
   _____

2. _____
   _____
   _____
   _____

3. _____
   _____
   _____
   _____

4. _____
   _____
   _____
   _____

5. _____
   _____
   _____
   _____

EXERCISE: YOUR ROLE IN THE HEALING PROCESS
(*continued*)

6. _____
_____
_____
_____

7. _____
_____
_____
_____

8. _____
_____
_____
_____

9. _____
_____
_____
_____

10. _____
_____
_____
_____

11. _____
_____
_____
_____

Ed's Story

What would you tell other partners?

The most difficult thing for me in being a partner was understanding—truly appreciating what she had been through without feeling cheated myself. Don't be judgmental. Try to get rid of any preconceived opinions about stories you've heard. Realize that you are dealing with your mate who has her own story. Educate yourself on the dynamics in this thing.

I could not picture someone living in a dynamic situation with all these powers being put on each person in the family. Pressures, expectations, shame, and guilt. Have an open mind and don't judge.

Sam's Story

Teamwork

It was nice in a way to be together or to think of yourself as a team when you're approaching this abuse thing. But I found it to be very difficult to say it's us against the world. It just seemed that she was so into herself and her own needs early in that period.

It was very tough to have that attitude of the "us" feeling; it seemed that so much was her. She couldn't explain a lot of it. She'd have memories and couldn't talk about. I felt it would have been nice to make a bond to deal with it at that level, but I don't think that ever really happened.

I think we do a better job communicating than we did two years ago. I think we understand a little better, are a little more cautious about what we say, and try and think ahead a little bit more. A lot of that I learned at the Trauma Center. How to deal with these situations, in some regard, has helped me to streamline my communication in trying to say what I mean and to respond appropriately. It can still be very difficult and at times having problems communicating is one of the things that starts to upset her the most.

As far as needs of intimacy, in general, she was very consumed with all of this, and it seemed to take up most of her effort, and there wasn't much to put forward during the first year. Now, it goes in spurts. There are times when we are close together and then we're away from each other again. I know there are times she goes through more flashback periods than others. I think she's getting to the point where she doesn't like to talk about it because she feels like everybody has heard this before.

I don't always know when she's going through this, but usually when she goes through one of these periods it makes our relationship more difficult. She's on edge and irritable, and any little thing can make her upset. I feel kind of pushed away. I react by backing into my shell and our intimacy level drops down. It varies, but it's not what it should be as far as I'm concerned.

I think she feels I can't do enough to show her my feelings or caring. If there were ten things I was supposed to do for her, errands or whatever, and I did nine and forgot one, she would be upset and think that I was selfish and didn't care. I feel incapable of doing enough to satisfy her moods and needs.

Four

The Survivor's Healing Process

Τhis chapter is a question-and-answer section about the survivor's healing process. The following are those questions most frequently asked by the partners of survivors:

- What is "the healing process"?
- How long will the healing process take?
- Will my mate ever be the same?
- How come survivors blame themselves for the abuse or rape?
- How come my spouse didn't tell me sooner?
- How come she hates men so much?
- How come this happened to my mate?
- How come my mate is always so moody?
- When can we make love again?
- How much more of this am I supposed to take?
- What can I do to help the survivor?
- How come I need a support group?

What is "the healing process"?

I first learned of this phrase through the works of Laura Davis, co-author with Ellen Bass of *The Courage to Heal* and author of *The Courage to Heal Workbook* and *Allies in Healing*. In Davis' workbook she describes the healing process as follows:

> Although there is no easy formula, there are
> certain recognizable stages survivors go through
> as they face the impact abuse has had on their
> lives. As you heal, you experience these stages
> repeatedly, each time with a different
> perspective and a greater sense of resolution.
> We called this the "healing process" or the spiral
> of healing.[1]

Throughout my training and schooling, I have found the term "healing process" to be widely accepted by both therapists and survivors. This term appropriately refers to the hard work, commitment, and growth that all survivors of incest, molestation, and rape go through.

The "healing process" for a survivor as utilized in my work involves the following:

- letting the survivor know it wasn't her/his fault

- allowing the client an opportunity to share her/his story in as safe a surrounding as can be provided

- giving the survivor a chance to openly express any and all emotions s/he presently feels or has difficulty expressing

---

[1] *Courage to Heal Workbook: For Women and Men Survivors of Child Sexual Abuse* (New York: Harper & Row, 1991), 3. This quotation is located in the section titled "About Language," in which Davis defines the word "partner" as anyone who has made an intimate commitment with the survivor.

- supporting the survivor's self-empowerment for regaining control in her/his life
- validating and normalizing the survivor's past and present feelings surrounding her/his victimization
- giving the survivor an opportunity to experience or re-experience her/his inner child (lost childhood, lost innocence)
- helping the survivor establish new coping strategies or mechanisms to replace those used during her/his victimization
- aiding the survivor in her/his inter- and intrapersonal relationships
- working on anger management
- aiding the survivor in eliminating self-destructive patterns and behaviors, e.g., substance abuse, suicidality, promiscuity, abusive relationships, and self-mutilation
- helping the survivor go through her/his grief and loss process
- establishing healthier ways of communicating
- exploring family issues, past and present
- working on self-esteem and a stronger sense of self

The above list is only a general representation of the areas I cover in a survivor's process to heal. Some, all, or additional areas can be covered depending on the survivor's needs and desires.

How long will the healing process take?

This was one of the most common questions asked when clients were interviewed for the partners group. The answer is that it takes as long as it takes. Sorry, but there just isn't a definitive answer for this question. From my experience with partners, this answer isn't good enough, especially when you feel like you are at the end of your rope. There are several reasons, however, why this question does not have an answer.

After any type of sexual victimization, the survivor will probably experience long-term effects. Some of the survivor's subsequent reactions to the abuse may occur sporadically at first, then dissipate over the course of the healing process. Or the survivor may experience other effects one year and not the next. For instance, s/he may not experience flashbacks until s/he begins counseling or may experience them only during physical intimate encounters with you.

Because life in general is ever changing, the survivor may not feel the impact from the abuse until years down the road. Perhaps the relationship the survivor now has with you will be the catalyst to certain reactions and behaviors s/he has not experienced before.

Another reason why the healing process cannot be restricted to a specific time frame is the suppression and/or repression of various feelings such as anger, shame, sadness, or grief. This defense or guarding of emotional expression is due to the discomfort and awkwardness in sharing feelings that have been hidden for long periods of time. Additionally, some emotions become more difficult than others to express at certain junctures of healing.

The survivor's healing process is often a lifetime of exploration into the impacts that the abuse has had. However, the victim of sexual abuse or rape doesn't become a survivor by her/his failures. S/he becomes a survivor by her/his strengths, which will now aid her/him in healing.

Will my mate ever be the same?

This, too, is a question without a definitive answer. Most definitely there will be changes in your mate, but there will also be differences in you and the relationship. It would be close to impossible for the survivor, you, and the relationship to remain unchanged. Whether the survivor is an adult recently raped or an adult who was molested as a child, changes will occur in many areas of her/his life.

This doesn't mean that the survivor and your relationship are forever devoid of intimacy, excitement, play, love, sex, fun, or anything else that you two have shared. In fact, the healing process may allow the survivor to grow and explore a part of her/himself that was forced into hiding.

The survivor's new sense of self will certainly become evident in her/his relationship with you. This process of discovery can initially seem a problem as you both struggle for a position in the relationship. This conflict is not isolated to relationships with survivors but can be a common theme in any intimate relationship.

As the partner, you too will have an opportunity for change and growth. In learning how to support your mate and yourself, you will be presented with opportunities for learning and discovering some things. You may find that this question is not just about the survivor "ever being the same" but also about you "ever being the same." This is why I encourage partners to seek out a support group and/or individual therapy while the survivor is working on her/his healing process.

How come survivors blame themselves for the abuse or rape?

With the survivors' self-blame comes the judgment that somehow they were at fault for their sexual assault or molestation. This belief stems from the concept that somehow they either asked for their victimization or were bad and deserved their abuse. From the rape survivors who think they should not have worn a particular outfit or to the molested children who think they were being disobedient to their parents, they all share the intrinsic belief that something as horrific as their victimization could only have occurred if they deserved it.

Along with self-blame comes shame, a sense of helplessness and hopelessness, and a feeling of worthlessness. The survivors' belief that they didn't do anything to prevent the molestation or assault keeps them in the role of victims and not survivors.

At times, friends, family members, the court system, and society as a whole often blame survivors for their victimization. This, too, only contributes to the survivors' guilt and shame over what happened.

How come my spouse didn't tell me sooner?

The decision of when to tell one's partner about a molestation or rape isn't about the partner as much as it is about the survivor. The decision of when to disclose a sexual assault is often based upon safety. Disclosing a traumatic event in one's life displays not only trust and courage but also vulnerability.

When partners ask this question, there are usually underlying feelings of hurt, rejection, disappointment, and anger. These emotions may arise in some partners who are not aware that a survivor's disclosures of her/his secrets are very painful experiences.

The adult survivor of childhood molestation has probably become quite accustomed to keeping her/his victimization a secret. This is something that survivors are forced into as they feel responsible for keeping the family together. Survivors often think that any disclosure of their abuse will only separate the family. They believe that if this happened, they would be the ones to blame, not their perpetrators.

Survivors may feel uncomfortable sharing the trauma because of the shame they feel in regard to their forced participation. Survivors of a sexual molestation may believe that they are now damaged or defective. With such terrible beliefs attached to being survivors, is there any wonder why they keep the secret?

Survivors of rape also have good cause to shelter their victimization. We have all heard of cases in which the victims are put on trial, not the rapists. Society often accuses rape victims of "wanting to be raped" because of the way they acted or dressed. Consequently, rape survivors feel betrayed by the legal system after the perpetrators are set free or receive only minimal sentences.

How come she hates men so much?

For the most part, perpetrators of sexual assaults and/or rapes are men. Having been victimized by men, a woman's ability to trust and feel safe becomes crucially compromised.

If you are a male partner, one of the toughest tasks you can "get a handle on" is to *not* take it personally when the survivor focuses her anger on men in general. Whether you are a partner of a rape survivor or incest survivor, you may find yourself caught in the direct line of a verbal assault merely because you are a man.

Most often, the attack on men is brought about by the survivor's attempt to get in touch with her anger for having been put through this trauma. Sometimes the survivor must begin by first generalizing this emotion toward all men. Only after her generalized anger subsides does she begin to direct her anger toward the actual perpetrator of the assault.

How come this happened to my mate?

Survivors are asking the same question: How come this happened to me? Yet, sadly, it remains unanswered. We live in a society often plagued by crime and violence. There are no guarantees that you, or a loved one, will not become victimized at some time. The victimization is never fair, and the road to healing is seldom an easy one. Remember that the survivor never asked to become the victim of a sexual assault or molestation but are left to bear its memory.

How come my mate is always so moody?

A term I often use when counseling survivors and partners is "emotional roller coaster." This term refers to the wide array of emotions a person feels after having experienced a traumatic event. It also refers to the highs and lows of how these emotions get expressed.

Emotions can be very difficult to communicate, especially when they have been hidden or defended. For the survivor of sexual molestation and/or rape, communicating emotions can be one of the toughest roads to travel on the healing journey.

Unresolved emotions from the victimization can cause the survivor's mood swings. Bottled-up feelings surface and can be explored more easily after the survivor learns to tell the story of her/his abuse or rape with an affective component.[2] In cases of early childhood molestation, some of these feelings may not have been experienced for many years or, sadly enough, ever at all.

The emotional roller coaster ride often begins once the survivor begins her/his healing process or as s/he begins to have flashbacks to the events of her/his sexual abuse or

---

[2] The affective component is the overt expression of emotion when a person speaks. Many survivors initially describe their victimization with no (flat) affect.

rape. When feelings begin to surface, they come through like a rushing flood. This causes the survivor to become scared, believing s/he will have no control over what s/he experiences.

During and after the attack, the survivor often utilizes many coping strategies to survive the terrible ordeal. These include, but are not limited to, denial, repression, dissociation, minimization, displacement, or rationalization of the perpetrator's behavior.

- **Denial**: blocking out painful realities
- **Repression**: rejecting and keeping out of consciousness painful experiences and/or that which causes elevated levels of anxiety
- **Dissociation**: separating, leaving the body; a method to keep pain and trauma away from awareness
- **Minimizing**: discounting in order to belittle or lessen
- **Displacement**: transferring affect to a substitute, placing feelings somewhere else
- **Rationalization**: making excuses or inventing reasons to free oneself from blame

When can we make love again?

Some partners I have worked with had to refrain from any sexual activity with their mates at the onset of the group. Others were able to maintain a sexual relationship with their mates up to the point of when the survivor began to have flashbacks. Various partners' sexual activities were on a stop-and-go basis. There is no steadfast answer.

Often the underlying issue becomes the loss of warmth and intimacy in the relationship. For these partners, other options for sharing intimacy were examined. Many partners found that they could maintain a high level of intimacy even though no intercourse was involved. Whether a couple used massage techniques, simple petting, cuddling, walks on the beach, dinners by candlelight, or hugs and kisses, they found ways to share in each others sensuality. Please refer to the chapter entitled "Intimacy."

How much more of this am I supposed to take?

A partner will usually ask this question more than once during the course of the survivor's road to healing. When you ask this question, you probably feel as if you are at the end of your rope. Perhaps you feel helpless and powerless about the outcome of your situation. Believe it or not, you can begin to understand much about the survivor's healing process when you ask yourself, "How much more of this am I supposed to take?"

The survivor could not control what her/his attacker(s) was or was not going to do to them. S/he also could not control how long the victimization would endure. A question many survivors ask themselves during, between, and after their victimizations is, "How much more of this can I take?" The answer is usually tied into what makes them as victims become survivors: defense mechanisms and coping strategies.

It helped the survivor to remember her/his strength and inner courage in surviving the trauma or abuse. Too often the survivor forgets or undermines the resourcefulness and abilities that allowed her/him to continue her/his life. Now, as the survivor works on the process to heal, s/he empowers her/himself by handling emotions that have been hidden since her/his victimization and subsequently adds new coping mechanisms.

As a partner, you will only be able to control your own actions, behaviors, and feelings about the relationship and its outcome. Though this will feel futile at times, it is not your responsibility to take on the feelings of your mate. Doing so will only cripple your process and the survivor's.

Work on your issues and allow your mate to work on her/his issues. By doing so, you will be able to find your own inner resourcefulness and coping strategies to deal with the present situation. This is how you are afforded opportunities to develop alternative ways to cope.

You can only do your best. Though many partners' stories are similar regarding their relationships, each person is different in her/his ability or willingness to work on her/his relationship. There is no right or wrong answer to the question, "How much more of this am I supposed to take?"

What can I do to help the survivor?

One of the very first things you can do to help support the survivor is to not try to take her/his pain away. The reality is that you can't do that, but you may desire to try anyway. For example, you may tell the survivor that everything is going to be fine. Regardless of the outcome down the road, telling a survivor that everything will be fine only minimizes the pain, hurt, and healing that s/he still feels and needs to work through. Remember, the survivor already tends to minimize her/his abuse.

Support the survivor by validating her/his feelings. Verbally acknowledge how terrible her/his victimization must have been. Listen carefully to what s/he says s/he feels and then express those feelings back to her/him. This not only supports the survivor but can also help stop the survivor's tendency to minimize her/his victimization.

Education is another important part of supporting the survivor. As a partner, you must educate yourself about what it means to be a survivor of rape or sexual molestation. The more you know, the less likely you will feel resentment. Many good books and articles on these topics are available, some of which are referenced in the chapter entitled "Resources."

You can also support the survivor by attending a support group for partners or by going to your own individual therapy. The reason for this is that you, too, will need to express your feelings and emotions surrounding the disclosure of the abuse. Your own therapy can normalize your process.

In any crisis or traumatic situation, a person must take care of her/himself before attempting to assist somebody else. Being a partner of a survivor who is actively working on her/his healing puts you in a situation as a resource for assistance. You must, however, take care of those pressing needs and feelings inside yourself and avoid suppressing them. It will be difficult for you to exhibit support for the survivor when you may not be able to support yourself through the trauma.

Keeping your emotions bottled up inside is only fuel for the fire of resentment toward the survivor. This doesn't mean that you should abandon the survivor and selfishly tend to your own needs and feelings. Strike a balance of tending to your own well-being and that of the survivor. How you feel is equally important in your relationship; it will be important for you to share your feelings and needs with the survivor as well. Just as you want to be there for her/him, s/he will want to be there for you. That's part of the teamwork that you must have as a couple.

Another key part of supporting a survivor is to avoid rushing her/his healing process. Remember the earlier question and answer of, "How long will the healing process take?" It takes as long as it takes. This means that you can't rush the survivor or yourself through the various stages of feelings.

Allow the survivor space, which can mean many different things. For example, space is giving the survivor a chance to ask for help before you offer it. This leads to empowerment of the survivor and helps her/him gain a sense of control. Space can be the freedom to experience various emotional states in a private setting, e.g., in a designated room in the house. Space can be a couple of hours to her/himself on a weekend. Space can be the time s/he wants to write in a journal or read some information s/he got from her/his support group. If you want to allow the survivor space for healing but you don't know what that means, ask her/him.

How come I need a support group?

You need a support group for the same reason that the survivor needs one: to have a safe place to express and share what's going on with you. Going to a support group allows you a chance to be selfish and to look at your needs.

One of the most common things partners share in the group experience is that they feel like they are walking on eggshells. It seems as though they cannot say or do anything without feeling guilty afterward. If this strikes a chord in you, then perhaps you see what makes the support group so important.

Support groups supply you with a place for questions, answers, and exploration. So many questions can remain unanswered for you. Having a place to go will help you explore new and different ways to handle being a partner.

Bill's Story

"The Healing Process"

For my wife, the healing process was having to get down into the depths and uncover all the buried feelings, memories, secrets, hidden garbage, anger, and denial of her own worth—to come to grips with it in a whole new way. She had to start reprogramming herself. She started going through positive affirmations and listening to tapes about loving herself.

My wife began to write about her feelings, the negative things she felt about herself, and how she wanted to feel about herself. She would then state, "I do feel that way about myself," "I do feel I am a good person," "I was not the one to blame for these situations," and "I'm lovable for who I am, not for my body."

She went through all sorts of different levels in confronting the misconceptions that were buried down inside her. Another thing that was important was to then share it with other people, those she could trust. I was one of those people.

I think even more important was her survivor support group. Hearing their stories reassured her that she wasn't alone out there. Being able to share her story allowed more feelings to come up and helped her to get to the truth of what really happened.

Until I came to an understanding of what she's been going through and what the healing process is, I really thought she was off the wall, taking it all a little too far, and making a big deal about nothing. It has been easier for me now that I gained some information about incest survivors. I no longer think she is off the wall.

Going through the healing process with my wife has probably brought us closer than we ever were. I think there were times when she wanted to give up on it, chuck it all away, maybe isolate, and get out of the relationship. There have been times when she would try to sabotage the relationship. I had to go beyond my needs and sacrifice them in order to allow her to go through certain stages.

It also got me more in touch with myself and my feelings. It's been very valuable. We went through some rocky times. It took a lot of commitment for both of us to get through those times. I'd say being honest has been very important in our relationship. It really enriched our relationship, going through this process together and her having my support through it.

Jack's Story

Male bashing

I don't know if I can live the rest of my life with someone who is constantly looking at the television and male bashing. When she sees a commercial on TV, like the Swedish Bikini Team in a beer commercial, she'll go nuts. She'll yell at the TV about the goddamn men who make these ads, sell women for skin and flesh, and the impact it has on kids.

I know she needs to get the anger out. She expressed why she was doing it, and that she had to do it. She said to please bear with her. Over a period of time I think she's definitely toned down her male bashing. It use to be that I would cringe when she'd say something about a commercial, but now I think we have a meeting of the minds. However, there are still times when I get fed up with it and say, "You're always blaming men for the ills of the world!"

I think she has to be appreciated and respected. That's the utmost thing in her mind right now. She has to be listened to and her opinions need to be valued. It comes down to respect. She has to feel that she's being treated fairly and loved and that she is not just thought of as a thing or an object. She's a living, breathing person with feelings and opinions and one who can add value. Another change I have noticed is she doesn't believe anyone; you have to prove everything to her. She won't believe me. It's like she's constantly doubting me. She has a lack of trust for people.

I need validation, too.

Every once in a while that little kid in me says, "Wait a minute, you should bail out of this. You should go off and do your own thing. You don't need all these headaches. Just get away from it." I am kind of torn there.

I appreciate having positive reinforcement, that I'm doing the right thing or not doing the right thing. She doesn't do that.

I think it's an appreciation for what I've gone through. To some extent it's been taken for granted. She has said to me on maybe two occasions over the past two or three years, "I know this has been rough for you. Thanks for hanging in there with me." I don't know what I'm expecting—maybe the sense that she has appreciated what I've gone through for her and for us.

Sam's Story

Anger!

I think she's angry about what she's gone through; memories come up. I think she has low self-esteem, and she is angry at the perpetrator. Any little thing that's a little bit out of whack during the day upsets her disproportionately. She doesn't feel that I care enough about her because we had marital problems just before this started.

The healing process for my wife was almost total confusion. My perception was that everything was slipping away from her, everything she knew. The linchpins of her whole sense of childhood. A sense of who she was was torn out from under her. She started to question those people and everyone around her. She had a sense of almost total bewilderment at first. Then I think it became anger as she became focused on what happened.

There was a tremendous amount of anger involved in this and a total sense of betrayal and worthlessness. She was told when she was a child that she deserved this. I don't know all the mechanics of her feelings now, but I think she felt tremendous anger, low self-esteem, and betrayal. It was to such an overpowering extent that it was very hard for her to function, like to get up or get the kids to school.

I think she feels that she's much better off than she was a year ago; she understands a lot better and is able to cope more with her feelings about the perpetrator and the anger. She's a lot better, but I think a lot of it is yet to surface.

The thought that she is going through a ton of things and still has a ton of things to go through before she can put this away and realize she's a worthwhile human being. She can feel proud of her accomplishments and so on.

Five

Grief and Loss

For a survivor of childhood molestation or a sexual assault, an important part of healing is the period of grief and loss. This refers to the time taken by the survivor to recognize and experience her/his denial, resentment, anger, pain, hurt, sadness, betrayal, and eventual acceptance of the losses s/he has experienced as a result of her/his victimization.

The adult survivor of childhood sexual molestation grieves the loss of childhood innocence. Often, the survivor of childhood sexual abuse is forced into growing up too fast. S/he plays the role of caretaker or custodian for the family. S/he may be manipulated and/or forced into handling many responsibilities, many of which are associated with that of a parental figure, e.g., caring for younger siblings (cooking, feeding, and bathing), tending to sick and ill family members, and keeping up both the inside and outside of the home.

A survivor even becomes caretaker for a parent who is the abuser. S/he makes sure, at any and all costs to her/himself, that the parent's needs are tended to, hoping that s/he, as the child victim, will no longer be violated. Trying to keep peace within the family is more than a full-time job for any adult, not to mention what it is to a child. In fact, for the child it becomes a no-win situation; it is impossible to maintain peace in an incestuous family.

To reiterate, the ultimate sacrifice for the traumatized youth becomes her/his childhood and innocence. Playtime becomes worktime. Carefree thoughts and playful things that other children have are only fantasy in the mind of the child survivor as s/he tries to maintain some type of hope or escape.

This sacrifice and loss of the simplicity of childhood will subsequently have to be grieved. The process is usually quite cumbersome; most often, the child does not have the opportunity to process the loss until s/he is physically out of the home. Sometimes the loss is pushed deep inside, and it isn't until years down the road that the survivor, as an adult, makes her/his first attempt at grieving.

The survivor of rape or attempted rape grieves the loss of internal and external safety in the world. Perhaps you have heard the expression, "looking at the world through rose-colored glasses." The survivor's ability to believe in her/his fellow human beings and even her/himself is shattered. The world is not a safe place! For the rape survivor, grieving is delayed until s/he breaks out of denial and moves past blaming her/himself for what happened.

The loss any survivor faces usually continues into her/his loving and intimate relationships. Your relationship and its inherent intimacy works as a catalyst to the survivor's self-exploration, usually through memory by association. The survivor may find that, in trying to keep up a full, healthy, and meaningful intimate relationship with you, s/he is forced into looking at unexplored losses in her/his life.

No matter what loss the survivor faces, her/his grieving process allows her/him to get in contact with many different feelings and reactions. However, the survivor may never have felt many of these sensations because they were repressed or were never appropriately demonstrated for her/him. Regardless, the survivor may never have experienced or dealt with these feelings on a conscious level.

As a partner, you, too, will have to work on grief and loss issues. An important part of your work will be to get a handle on the feelings associated with grieving and then effectively experience and channel them when they arise. That you are experiencing a loss may come as a shock to you, but take a moment to examine some of the following predicaments shared by other partners:

- It feels like I'm walking on eggshells. I must always watch what I say and do.
- A lot of the time I stuff what is going on inside of me.
- I have to refrain from sexual contact with my mate.
- We don't go out socially as much as we used to.
- My mate never seems to initiate sex.
- We don't see some of our old friends, and I hardly get to see my mate's family anymore.
- I rarely get to hear how thoughtful I am.
- The relationship doesn't have the same level of intimacy as it used to have.
- We used to cuddle and hold hands a lot. Now, sometimes I can't hug or caress my mate.
- My mate isn't very supportive of me.
- We don't have as much fun now as we did earlier in our relationship.

These are losses, and you must allow yourself the necessary time to grieve them. However, just recognizing the loss in your relationship is insufficient for you to appropriately move on. From my experience in working with partners, if you don't do your own grief work and bring your feelings to the surface, you will begin to feel resentment toward your mate. Eventually, you won't just blame the perpetrator but the survivor as well for making you have to deal with this "stuff."

Deciding when it is the right time to grieve is never an easy decision. Excuses and rationalizations come easily as you attempt to avoid the work underneath the loss. Perhaps you fear that the loss will be emotionally draining and too cumbersome for your already overwhelmed emotional state.

You may assume that you are too angry to get in touch with other feelings such as sadness and loss. You may even avoid grieving because you believe it to be useless, a waste of time, a futile attempt to change things, or a cause of only more problems for you. Perhaps you attempt to push your feelings far enough down, suppressing any invasive thoughts and expecting not to worry about it. This isn't a permanent or healthy solution. In time, your body and mind will hold no more, and that repressed energy will come out in other forms. Here are some examples of how your body and mind will release unresolved grief and loss:

- physical symptoms and ailments (headaches, stomachaches, muscle tension, frequent colds or flu)
- depression
- short temper
- high level of frustration at work or play
- low tolerance for handling day-to-day situations
- problems in communication
- interpersonal relationship difficulties
- heightened sensitivity to feeling rejected or vulnerable

You will only go so far in your process and relationship before the decision to mourn or not surfaces again. The next time the issue comes up it will probably manifest itself in an emotion such as anger, resentment, disappointment, hopelessness, or frustration.

EXERCISE: GRIEF AND LOSS

The following exercise will help you get in touch with some of the losses you have had or are presently experiencing as a partner. While doing the exercise, besides simply recognize the loss, become aware of the feelings that come up.

Take the next ten to fifteen minutes to think about some of the relevant changes that have occurred in your relationship with your mate. Write each change down. After the time has elapsed, arrange them according to most significant to least significant.

Changes that have occurred in my relationship:

1. _____

2. _____

3. _____

4. _____

5. _____

6. _____

7. _____

8. _____

9. _____

10. _____

11. _____

WRITING EXERCISE: GRIEF AND LOSS

From your list in the previous exercise, select one change and take the next fifteen to twenty minutes to write about it. Do not be concerned with what you write; just let your thoughts, feelings, and pen flow. Upon completion of your writing, read it aloud to yourself. You might be surprised by some of the bottled-up feelings you have.

Try to utilize this exercise for each of the items on your hierarchy as well as any additional losses that come to mind. You will achieve better results if you write about only one of these at a time. Complete the exercise at your own pace; take a few days or a couple of weeks. The important thing is that you get in touch with your loss or losses.

When you are comfortable, bring any feelings that came up in your writing into your own therapy or group meeting. I have found that when partners share their losses and the feelings surrounding them, it has a normalizing sensation. You are not alone in your grief.

_____

_____

_____

_____

_____

_____

_____

WRITING EXERCISE: GRIEF AND LOSS (*continued*)

_____

_____

_____

_____

_____

_____

_____

_____

_____

_____

_____

_____

_____

_____

_____

_____

_____

WRITING EXERCISE: GRIEF AND LOSS (*continued*)

_____

_____

_____

_____

_____

_____

_____

_____

_____

_____

_____

_____

_____

_____

WRITING EXERCISE: GRIEF AND LOSS (*continued*)

_____

_____

_____

_____

_____

_____

_____

_____

_____

_____

_____

_____

_____

_____

Six

Communication

I will begin this chapter by sharing two definitions, each of which is taken from *The New Lexicon Webster's Dictionary of the English Language* (New York: Lexicon Publications, Inc., 1987):

- **Communication**: a sending, giving, or exchanging (of information, ideas, etc.); a method of such exchange

- **Communication gap**: a failure to convey and/or understand the information, intent, or meaning of another, especially between individuals of different perception

Communicating is something we have been doing since we were infants wanting attention, food, or maybe just to be held. As an adult, our tools for communication are not as primitive, yet at times we forget how to effectively "send, give, or exchange" what we are feeling. We also tend to forget how to allow someone else the opportunity to communicate her/his "information, ideas, etc."

The term "communication gap" has been around for quite a few years and is well recognized for describing the inability of one's generation to be understood by the older generation. As a partner of a survivor, you may believe there is a communication gap in your relationship. Both you and the survivor may believe there is a mutual "failure to convey and/or understand the information, intent, or meaning" of the other. At times you will both realize that your perceptions of situations or events that occur in the relationship are quite different.

This chapter is designed to provide a foundation for better communication skills. The ability to communicate your thoughts and feelings to the survivor and vice versa will be vital in maintaining your relationship. A breakdown in communication is usually the first problematic area in any relationship, with sequential effects branching into other areas. At the end of this chapter you will find exercises for learning how to effectively communicate with each other.

During the communication process, particularly when it involves a difference of opinion, you and the survivor will often fall victim to many different pitfalls. These include, but are not limited to, mind reading, interrupting, yelling and screaming, name calling, bringing up past issues, experiencing reactions and defensiveness toward each other, pushing each other's buttons, and blaming and finding fault with each other. Any combination of or even one pitfall can escalate a simple disagreement into an all-out, no-holds-barred argument.

You may find yourselves doing battle to the point of taking verbal "potshots" or "hitting below the belt." Compromise and resolution are no longer your goals; the attempt at communication becomes a matter of winning or losing. During these heated arguments, it might seem easier and more productive to strike back rather than attempt an understanding of your mate's point of view. There are, however, ways to avoid this "win or lose" mindset in communicating.

One way to properly communicate thoughts and feelings is to consider how you phrase your statements and questions. Take a look at the following examples of some statements and questions and how they are phrased.

- "You're pissed off again, aren't you?"
- "It was your fault that happened."
- "You really hurt me when you said that!"
- "I know how you are feeling right now."
- "You always have to get the last word in!"
- "Don't make me feel guilty over what happened."

Now consider the following examples with the use of "I" statements and questions.

- "I wonder if you are feeling angry at me."
- "I think we are both responsible for what happened."
- "I feel hurt by what was said."
- "I wonder what you are feeling now."
- "I get the sense that it is important for you to be heard. Is that true?"
- "I'm feeling guilty and bad over what happened."

Note the differences between the first and the second set of statements. The second set of examples aren't accusatory and don't attempt to place blame on the person hearing the phrases. They also don't imply that you know exactly how your mate is feeling. Do not try to label what someone else is feeling. Perhaps you think you have a good idea about how the survivor might be feeling or how you would feel in that situation. However, you really can't read your mate's mind; therefore, telling the survivor how s/he is feeling (angry, sad, or hurt) is only giving an opinion: your opinion.

Granted, the survivor's behaviors can give you clues about how s/he might feel. The point remains that, for proper communication to occur, you don't *tell* your mate how s/he feels. By using statements such as, "I get the impression that you might be feeling...," "It sounds as if you are feeling...," or "I wonder if you might be feeling...," you allow yourself an opportunity to check in with the survivor.

The statements and questions in the second set also indicate the speaker taking responsibility for her/his own feelings and actions. These types of statements are far less intrusive and do not put the survivor on the defensive because you haven't told her/him how s/he is feeling. The survivor has an opportunity to agree or disagree with you.

Proper communication must also allow for a time of "give and take." This means that only one person can speak at a time. Allow time to talk and time to listen; otherwise you get stuck in a shouting match. In fact, when you find that each of you is trying to out-talk or talk over the other, you tend to *react* to the conversation, not *act*. Reacting, instead of independently acting upon what the other says, puts the control outside of yourself. As you react, you become defensive and place responsibility for your feelings on the other person.

Communication can also be aided by asking each other questions. In the communication process, questions are useful tools in a few different ways. First, they can clarify unclear issues. Second, they help you avoid the pitfall of mind reading and using an overactive imagination. Questions also get you both more involved in an exchange of information and ideas instead of a debate over who is right and who is wrong.

Of all the useful elements in proper communication, validation can be the most helpful. When you validate what the other person has expressed to you, s/he will believe that s/he was listened to and not just heard. Validation means you acknowledge the other point of view, not that you agree or approve of it. You are letting the other person know that you are there with her/him as s/he expresses what is on her/his mind. Validating the other tells her/him that you are attentive to what he has to say because you subsequently reflect back what s/he just expressed. To reflect back or paraphrase what the other person just stated, you do not repeat word for word what was said. Reflecting back only the content will make you seem robotic in your attempt to validate. You must include the affective component—that is, the emotional content and "feelings" just stated to you.

A survivor's ability to openly express how s/he feels is probably a new concept for her/him. More often than not, adults abused as children were often forced into "stuffing" not only what they wanted to say but also their feelings. In addition, an abused child usually has poor role models for learning how to effectively communicate.

Rape survivors are also forced into a position of keeping silent. During an attack, they are often threatened with violence and physical harm, even with being killed. Add to this the shame that so often comes with being a survivor of rape, and the ability to express feelings becomes guarded and difficult. This does not mean that survivors do not or cannot communicate just as effectively as non-survivors. Remember, at some point(s) in the survivor's life, the ability to openly express her/himself was taken from her/his control.

As a partner, try to avoid putting the survivor in a similar situation. That does not mean the survivor gets to take away your ability to openly communicate. You must strike a balance, and each of you must at least allow for a forum to communicate your feelings and needs.

EXERCISE: COMMUNICATION #1

The purpose of the following exercise is to assist you in learning how to reflect back what your mate has just expressed to you. A good way to start practicing this exercise is by telling each other how your day went.

1. To begin, start out with small sentences. When the first mate is done speaking, the other mate must reflect back what was said. The objective is *not* to repeat word for word what was said. Try to reflect back not just the content but the feelings and emotions expressed by the person speaking.

2. Next, the mate who originally spoke states whether the reflection was correct or incorrect. If it was correct, switch roles and take turns practicing how to reflect back. If the reflection was not correct, find out what feelings and emotions were not acknowledged and try it again.

If you work together on this exercise, you can both benefit by learning how to listen and reflect back what the other mate says. Once you have both completed this exercise with a certain regularity in reflecting each other's feelings, move on to other areas of conversation. Once each of you becomes comfortable with how your mate is reflecting back statements, it might become easier to share deeper, more intimate thoughts.

EXERCISE: COMMUNICATION #2

This exercise will help you talk out your disagreements in a more structured format. By setting aside designated amounts of time for talking and listening, you allow an equal opportunity for each of you to share your feelings and for each mate to hear the other person's side. Take some time as a couple to set up boundaries so that each of you will feel comfortable.

For example, choose ten minutes to express your side of the story as well as any feelings that come up. After each ten-minute interval, allow two to three minutes for the other mate to reflect back. Go back and forth as often as needed or set up a time limit for how much time you both want to dedicate to the conflict.

You don't necessarily have to resolve the disagreement. The intent is that you each learn to set up boundaries and try to avoid talking over each other. You will be surprised at the results this exercise might have in preventing disagreements from turning into full-blown arguments. Allow for a balance of time.

WRITING EXERCISE: COMMUNICATION #3

This exercise will help you learn how to show empathy for your mate while communicating with her/him. Empathy is a vital ingredient in effective communication. Empathy is the ability to put yourself in another person's shoes and truly hear what s/he says without passing judgment as s/he expresses it. You do not have to agree with what is said or even like it, but hear her/his side without attacking her/him.

Note: This exercise can be very difficult to do, especially when you are in disagreement with your mate. If you are not in a comfortable place to be in your mate's shoes, then now is not the time to work on this exercise.

Think back to a recent disagreement or argument you had with your lover. For the moment, set aside your opinion and feelings on the issue. Now, try to imagine what your mate's side of the encounter was. Put yourself in her/his shoes.

Do not pass judgment on her/his side of the story, but try to identify what her/his feelings and needs might have been in that situation. Do this as a freestyle writing exercise. Allow yourself ten to fifteen minutes to write about things from your mate's perspective.

When the time has passed, carefully read what you have written. Sometimes, by putting yourself in someone else's shoes, you can communicate more clearly. This doesn't mean you lose your perspective on the issues; you are merely aware of the flip side of the coin.

WRITING EXERCISE: COMMUNICATION #3 (*continued*)

_____

_____

_____

_____

_____

_____

_____

_____

_____

_____

_____

_____

_____

_____

WRITING EXERCISE: COMMUNICATION #3 (*continued*)

_____

_____

_____

_____

_____

_____

_____

_____

_____

_____

_____

_____

_____

Seven

Intimacy

As the mate of a survivor going through the healing process, you will encounter changes in the intimacy level of your relationship. These changes can come about slowly or drastically. No matter how dramatic or small the change, it will seem like a significant modification. This, too, becomes an area for exploration and growth in your relationship with the survivor.

Intimacy is not limited to your sexual relationship but includes the emotional bond you feel toward each other. Many partners from the support groups refer to the change in their intimate relationship as a break in emotional closeness. This closeness or intimacy takes on many different forms and meanings in your relationship.

Your thoughts and feelings on intimacy can be associated with special situations, periods of time, memories, feelings, or thoughts unique to you and your mate. The following list contains examples of how intimacy manifests itself in a relationship:

- how you interact as a couple
- how you speak (communicate) to each other
- use of affectionate pet names
- ease with which you trust each other

- dating
- thoughts of each other when you are apart
- friendship
- non-sexual touch
- ability to make each other laugh
- how you play together
- raising a family together
- support and help you lend each other
- sharing of common interests
- ability to fulfill some of your mate's needs
- fantasies and dreams you share
- making love together

All of these examples and more add up to the level of intimacy you share in your relationship. What, then, are some of the contributing causes that create change in the relationship and its level of intimacy with a survivor?

To answer this question you must first look at the crucial element of intimacy: trust—not just the willingness to trust but also the ability. Trust is paramount in the survivor's decision to become emotionally connected to you.

As discussed earlier, the survivor's capacity to trust was radically reduced when s/he was sexually assaulted or molested. Whether s/he was violated as a child by trusted authority figures or raped as an adult, her/his ability to trust became severely compromised. Therefore, you must assume the position of a sensitive, empathetic mate so that the survivor can begin to recapture the ability to trust again.

Time and counseling usually lessen the difficulty in letting down protective barriers. By dealing with the underlying sadness, hurt, disappointment, anger, and loss involved with tainted trust, survivors begin to empower and strengthen themselves to trust again. This doesn't mean, however, that they will completely forget how their ability to trust was originally tarnished.

Additionally, survivors may not be willing to forgive themselves for having been so trusting. This is an important issue because with molestation, incest, or rape comes self-blame. Survivors tend to chastise themselves, believing they should have known better. They question why they ever trusted this person who covertly was a perpetrator.

Physical safety is also a concern for survivors. Their perception of safety becomes altered. Will their bodies ever be safe in future familial, social, or work situations? Having experienced such a violation(s) of boundaries, survivors aren't ready to let down their guard in a future intimate relationship without some resistance.

The relationship's level of intimacy also changes due to the flood of emotions that each of you are attempting to vent and express. It is not easy to express warmth and love when you are dealing with feelings of resentment and anger toward each other. Partners will also feel hurt, rejected, and neglected. As you struggle to handle these feelings, you may feel awkward expressing the love you still hold for your mate.

Another reason intimacy changes is the belief in old stereotypes that say intimacy is expressed primarily through a sexual relationship. Many people are still unaware that intimacy can be expressed in other ways. Without exploring other approaches to sharing your love for each other, the degree of intimacy gets stigmatized according to how your sexual relationship is. Subsequently, survivor and partner are set up for disappointment and emotional distancing.

To help increase the level of intimacy in your relationship, you need to rekindle the romance. You could brainstorm expressions of intimacy in support group settings, but most of the ways to rekindle intimacy have to come from you and the survivor as a couple. As the relationship becomes void of intimacy, change and creativity are often the sparks you need to re-ignite what was once there.

Whether you try going back to dating, holding hands, or going away for a special weekend at a favorite resort, together you must find ways to rediscover your passion for each other. Think back to the time when you courted each other; what things were important and unique to you as a couple? Many partners and survivors have shared that they created a better and stronger emotional bond by finding new ways to rekindle their romance.

Massage is a technique that uses touch for couples struggling with a loss of intimacy. Below are three types of massage—Swedish, reflexology, and aromatherapy;[1] you may wish to try one or all three or select another type. A brief summary paragraph introduces each type of massage; you can explore them further by checking out books on the topic, some of which are listed in the "Resources" section of this book.

Swedish Massage

Swedish massage involves five different techniques:

1. Effleurage: the stroking of muscles toward the heart. Use whole surface of palms and fingers. Helps to soothe muscles.

2. Petrissage: a circular kneading of muscles with both hands simultaneously. Increases cellular and nerve activity.

3. Friction: a deep circular manipulation with tips of thumbs or fingers, slipping them in a back and forth motion over the skin rapidly. Manipulates stiff joints and brings blood to area. Commonly used for sciatica, fractures, spasms, or sprains.

4. Tapotement: a percussion movement using both hands alternately with loose wrists in a rhythmic

---

[1] Massage definitions supplied by Pamela J. Sillman, CPFT, CMT.

fashion. Used before an athletic event or for bronchial problems.

5. Vibration: a fine shaking movement made by hands or fingers placed firmly against a body part to cause it to vibrate. Helps inflamed nerves.

Reflexology

Reflexology is a massage that applies pressure to one of three areas: the feet, hands, or ears. Special techniques are utilized through the thumb, finger, or hand. Lotions and oils are not used. Reflexology can aid the immune system by helping the body heal itself and can assist in stress reduction. Reflexology is also said to increase self-confidence.

Aromatherapy

The most common associations with aromatherapy are perfumes and fragrances. Aromatherapy utilizes massage and oils to work with various body organs and their functions. It is thought that this type of massage works not only on a physical level but also on an emotional one. Aromatherapy is based on the principle that all people have a scent of their own that varies depending on their diverse states of being.

The exercise at the end of this chapter helps enable couples to physically and emotionally connect—with or without having sexual intercourse. Two important ingredients in this exercise are communication and setting and respecting boundaries.

Communication is a vital ingredient in intimacy. Each of you must be able to communicate what you want and what you don't want in terms of an intimate relationship.

You may find you have certain needs your mate cannot presently fulfill. To help avoid confusion, resentment, and complications, you both must communicate your thoughts and feelings. For specific information on how to effectively communicate, please refer to the chapter, "Communication."

The second ingredient, setting and respecting boundaries, is imperative in trying to break new ground in your intimate relationship. Having read the earlier part of this chapter and the previous chapters, you are now somewhat familiar with how the survivor's ability to trust may have been grossly compromised. Be a patient partner in this regard. The survivor's trust in self and others can be regained through hard work, time, and setting and respecting boundaries.

Setting boundaries involves each of you going at a comfortable pace in the following exercise. Couples make their biggest mistake in the intimacy exercise when they stop taking small steps—for example, jumping from a simple massage with clothes on to sexual intercourse during the same encounter.

Remember: the purpose of this exercise is to develop a deeper and more meaningful expression of touching and loving on emotional and physical levels, *not* to manipulate your way into having sex. Do not proceed to the next step until it feels right and safe for both of you.

The exercise works best when you mutually decide on the appropriate time to move to the next step. If you find yourselves at different places, that's okay. Take the time to explore how each of you is feeling. This, too, is part of the exercise and can lead to a better and deeper understanding of your intimate needs.

I suggest that both partner and survivor read the exercise in its entirety before attempting any of the steps. By reading the exercise through, you each have the opportunity to note which step(s) might be worked more slowly or discussed in greater length before proceeding. As you work through the steps, feel free to follow any of the listed suggestions or create your own.

One last word of caution: This exercise is not designed to work on sexual dysfunctions or sexual problems of either a physical and/or psychological nature. If you are concerned with any of these areas, I recommend consulting a medical doctor, sex therapist, and/or your own therapist. This exercise is designed only for those couples who choose to work on issues of physical closeness and trust surrounding their intimate relationship.

EXERCISE: INTIMACY

Step One

Explore and research the different types of massage. Remember, massage can be utilized for many different things, such as:

- emotional release

- stress reduction

- sleep

- relaxation

- reduction of muscle tension or soreness

- exercise warm up or cool down

- foreplay to sexual intimacy

- sexual dysfunctions

- non-sexual intimacy

- spirituality

- rewarding oneself (for a new job, promotion, finished task, graduation, etc.)

It's okay to start with a specific massage or technique and then decide to change; don't stick with your original decision if the selected massage becomes uncomfortable for you or your mate. This is only the beginning of your journey toward learning about each other's likes and dislikes.

Suggestion: Some of the partners I have worked with took the approach of scheduling a date around their first step.

EXERCISE: INTIMACY (*continued*)

Step Two

Once you have found a comfortable massage technique that fits both of your needs, set some rules and boundaries surrounding its application. Decide who will massage whom first. How long will the massage last? Do you want to start by massaging only certain muscle groups?

Some couples like to start with a simple basic massage of the neck and shoulders. One person may prefer to have just the feet massaged or perhaps to have her/his mate brush her/his hair and massage the scalp. These, too, can be part of the intimate experience.

Remember, each of you must set your own boundaries about what you feel comfortable with. This includes not only what area(s) you choose to have massaged but also what area(s) you are comfortable in massaging on the other person. What do *you* want? You might also outline when and where on your body the next massage will take place. The purpose is not to put restrictions on your exploration but to create an environment of trust and safety.

During this step, talk to each other about sensitive and safe areas on your bodies. Are there areas of your body that you would rather not have massaged at this or any other time? The partner does not need to know why an area is off limits for the survivor. Just accept that it is off limits. The choice to disclose any information about sexual molestation or assault always remains with the survivor.

Another key element in this step is taking time-outs. Create a word, phrase, or sign to use when either of you needs to stop the activity you are engaged in. This time-out must be respected by each of you because it enables the person who

EXERCISE: INTIMACY (*continued*)

takes the time-out to take control of what s/he presently feels or is reacting to.

Suggestion: Write down any rules, limits, boundaries, areas of your body you don't want touched, your time-out phrase, and anything else that either of you believes is important in this exercise. This helps avoid questions or discrepancies that might arise down the road; it will help facilitate a safe environment for exploration in a highly sensitive area.

Step Three

This step is the first attempt at physical contact with your mate. Remember, take small steps here; do not jump the gun. Try not to massage any area that your mate may consider sexually stimulating. Initially, you might want to leave some or all of your clothes on before proceeding to massage directly on the skin.

Try to focus only on what it feels like to be massaged or to give the massage. If you are the recipient of the massage, don't worry about your mate becoming tired or about the massage becoming tedious or boring.

If the mate giving the massage gets into the art of massage and listens to the requests of the receiver, you will not only minimize clock watching but really get in tune with your mate's body. When you hear a request to "move a little to the left" or "press down a little heavier," accommodate your mate's request.

EXERCISE: INTIMACY (*continued*)

There are two important things you should remember during Step Three:

1. If, during the massage, either the receiver or giver becomes sexually aroused, you have no obligation to satisfy the arousal of your mate. Such a sense of obligation can lead to anger, resentment, and guilt. If the sexual arousal of your mate or yourself feels threatening, take a time-out. Rather than act on the sexual arousal or pass judgment on the reason for sexual arousal, take time to process what each of you is feeling at that moment.

2. Try not to get too caught up in the moment and lose touch with the boundaries and limits you have set. You may want to schedule separate times for massage and sexual intimacy. Of course you can have intercourse when the mood arises; however, remember that, at this step, the massage is not being used as foreplay. Perhaps once you are both more comfortable around sex and how it fits into your relationship, you may choose massage as foreplay. Keep communicating throughout this step.

You do not have to take the next step for the intimacy exercise to be useful. Only take Step Four if together you want to develop, enhance, or explore sexual intercourse.

EXERCISE: INTIMACY (*continued*)

Step Four (optional)

Begin this step when and if you are both fully comfortable with giving and receiving massages to areas not sexually stimulating. Do not proceed to Step Four if the survivor is experiencing flashbacks associated with physical touch. This step will involve massaging areas you previous avoided because they were sexually arousing; probability of the survivor experiencing a flashback is therefore increased. Remember to listen to any requests from the receiver of the massage and to honor the boundaries set. Proceed slowly. Communicate.

Suggestion: You cannot read each other's mind, so use the time-out as needed. If the survivor has a flashback, give her/him space. S/he will probably know best what s/he needs to do to take care of her/himself. Perhaps the survivor needs some time to get in touch with her/his emotions, or s/he may need to be held and have her/his feelings validated. If you are unsure about what you can do to assist the survivor, ask her/him.

Eight

Sex and Making Love

Sex can take on many different roles in any relationship:

- a way of expressing a certain level of intimacy
- an act to gain control and power
- a channel for releasing stress
- an element of a fantasy
- a method of making up
- a means to satisfy a physical and biological urge
- the means for reproduction

Regardless of how and what sex is used for in your relationship, it may have a different meaning for each of you at different times.

The pleasure and joy of making love to your significant other plays an important part in any intimate relationship. It is no different when the relationship involves a survivor and a partner. Each of you will have some sexual desires and needs that you choose to share with your lover. When these desires and needs come up, each of you must help establish an atmosphere of safety in which to discuss and/or act upon those needs and desires. The ability and freedom for each of you to express the option of saying "yes" or "no" during a discussion and/or act of making love helps foster greater trust.

The role that sex plays in your relationship with the survivor will assuredly go through changes. You may find that not only the survivor's ability but also her/his desire to have sex will drop off considerably or completely for short and/or long periods of time. The survivor's need and want to refrain from sexual activity usually isn't because of anything you did or didn't do. Ordinarily, abstinence from sexual activity is caused by the survivor's earlier abuse or rape.

Regardless of how sensitive and compassionate you may be as a lover, the survivor will sometimes feel the need to shut down either partially or completely. Survivors choose to protect themselves in any number of ways, including complete abstinence from sexual activity, shutting down their feelings during sex, rushing through a sexual encounter, or becoming unable to reach orgasm. (The inability to reach orgasm can be physical, psychological, or a combination of both. This should be looked into by the appropriate healthcare professionals.)

Many partners have shared that they needed a sense of hope regarding the future of their sexual relationship. Hope is not born out of the ultimatum, "Discontinue the abstinence or the relationship is over"; hope comes with accepting that, for now, sexual intercourse is one missing part of the relationship; it is not within the partner's control and can be restored.

Without ulterior motives, support for the survivor's boundaries and patience in helping to create a safe environment for sexual exploration can initiate or return you to a physically and emotionally stimulating sex life.

When partners were asked to describe their present sexual relationships, most of them stated that there were some definite differences once the survivor began working on her/his healing process. You may find that your sexual relationship is affected in one or more of the following ways:

- the frequency of sex
- the variety of sexual activity
- the emotional bond before, during and after making love
- the ability to talk openly about sex

You may also lose another element in your sexual relationship: the ability to be spontaneous with your desires. You may think that any attempt to make love spontaneously with your mate will only exacerbate her/his trauma. You might think that to act on a sexual desire or need is the same as a perpetrator's act to victimize and control. By wanting to make love to your mate at the spur of the moment and on impulse, are you now no less of a perpetrator?

In regard to sexual spontaneity, you must recognize the choices you have in taking responsibility for your own feelings, needs, and desires. The ability to *not* force your wants and wishes on another person shows the ability to respect her/his boundaries. There is nothing wrong with wanting to make spontaneous love to your mate. Forcing your mate to respond to your desires and needs is what you need to question.

WRITING EXERCISE: SEX AND MAKING LOVE

This exercise is designed to help you understand what your motives and underlying feelings are when you become aroused and wish to spontaneously act on your sexual impulse with your lover. The exercise is not intended to squelch the desire to make love spontaneously; rather it is intended to help you explore feelings and emotions that you might otherwise miss.

Use the following writing exercise the next time you feel the need to act spontaneously on a sexual desire but are afraid to approach your mate for fear of guilt, rejection, or retaliation.

Write about your fantasy. Describe how it feels to have this urge to act spontaneously with your mate. Include as much detail as you feel comfortable writing about. Let your mind and thoughts flow freely, including how your sexual encounter with your mate turns out. Be sure to include the feelings that come up for you before, during, and after the fantasy.

_____

_____

_____

_____

_____

_____

WRITING EXERCISE: SEX AND MAKING LOVE
(*continued*)

_____

_____

_____

_____

_____

_____

_____

_____

_____

_____

_____

_____

_____

_____

_____

_____

_____

WRITING EXERCISE: SEX AND MAKING LOVE
(*continued*)

_____

_____

_____

_____

_____

_____

_____

_____

_____

_____

_____

_____

_____

_____

Bill's Story

What about love and intimacy?

She wasn't getting through it as fast as I'd like her to. I still had needs that weren't getting met. I felt very frustrated and angry. I didn't know whether I'd be able to get my needs met in the situation.

In my group sessions we started dealing with techniques of communication, sensitivity, intimacy, and physical touching. Both of us started gaining more trust with each other physically. My wife was able to be very specific about what she needed to get intimate. To even think of making love she wanted to know about it beforehand, like setting a date. At first I was angry about that. Where was the spontaneity in our relationship and sexuality?

Finally, I was able to accept the fact that she needed to set specific dates and times for when we were going to make love. I could live with that. It helped to get my needs met, and it was a step in getting our relationship and intimacy intact. We were able to grow and learn more about one another and the situation.

Jack's Story

Needs

Initially, our sexual relationship changed in that she was physically bruised. I made a commitment to myself that I wasn't ever going to approach her until I felt comfortable that she wouldn't be offended by it. My wife also used to like when I would buy her lingerie and sexy outfits, but since the attack she just totally refused to wear them.

She felt it made women look like whores and that it was all part of American society: the marketing of women for sex and not for who they really are. So she just totally stopped wearing anything even if it was just a silk top. It kind of indirectly had an impact on our sex life because I liked that, and it was arousing to see. I never really told her that.

Nine

Anger

Anger is perhaps one of the most difficult emotions to express in ourselves and or to acknowledge in someone else. Anger is an emotion that all too often gets misdirected, repressed, shut off, projected, displaced, minimized, rationalized, denied, and mismanaged.

The difficulty and awkwardness in expressing anger can make it seem like a double-edged sword. The ability, however, to come face-to-face with anger and express it appropriately is often a crucial part of the survivor's healing process. As a partner, you will also find this to be a decisive part of your work and growth.

One thing I have noticed about the majority of partners is that they seem to recognize the survivor's anger before their own. Do you find this to be true of yourself? If so, this can be attributed to your perception that you are an active and ongoing target for the survivor's rage. Over and above this, you may be aware of your own anger but for fear of retribution, guilt, or blame choose not to acknowledge it openly.

Admitting your own anger (as well as other emotions) can be difficult when you are spending your energy on claiming responsibility for the survivor's feelings. The survivor enables this process, causing the two of you to enter into an unwritten agreement of taking responsibility for how the other feels. Each of you may feel unhappy, frustrated, and helpless about this exchange, yet you stay in the cycle.

You stand a better chance of being heard and of understanding your mate by taking responsibility only for your feelings. To do this, change must take place, which may seem scary and unsafe. Taking responsibility for your own feelings also means examining yourself more closely, which also can bring about fear.

People have other reasons why they choose not to accept responsibility for their anger. For instance, anger is often associated with fault or blame because of something said or done. Consequently, we say, "You made me get mad," which is easier than saying, "I'm feeling angry at what happened."

Perhaps you link your feelings of anger with insensitivity toward the survivor and her/his victimization. As a result of this connection, you find yourself feeling guilty for harboring this emotion. You assume that to be a more supportive and understanding partner, it would be better to stuff your anger rather than express it. In time, however, your repressed anger turns into feelings of depression or resentment. You may even find yourself holding onto the anger until it eventually escalates, causing you to reach a breaking point. Ultimately, you explode at the survivor, creating the very confrontation you tried to avoid.

Expressing your anger only after it escalates merely exacerbates your fears in coming to terms with it. This process of holding onto anger makes it seem unmanageable and brings about other concerns and questions. Did you create a threatening environment for future communication? Are you or your mate now experiencing a fear of abandonment? Does the expression of your anger lead you to conclude that it is only abusive and harmful?

Regardless of how you presently deal with your anger or the survivor's anger, it takes time to cope and handle it differently. You must first become aware of what you want to change and then have an alternative plan, action, or behavior available. Only then can change begin to happen. What might be some alternatives for when you get angry?

Some recommendations include releasing anger through a physical activity such as jogging, walking briskly, bike riding, doing aerobics, or weightlifting. These activities allow the adrenaline rush often synonymous with feelings of anger being released. Another option is taking a time-out and going to a quiet spot somewhere away from the "heated situation." The time-out option gives you an opportunity to come back later to explore your feelings.

Additional alternatives include screaming and yelling into a pillow or cushion, hitting a punching bag or a bed, practicing various breathing exercises, or trying to alleviate the tension associated with anger by working on relaxation exercises. Some options work better than others in certain situations. You will know what works best for you. What is important is that you find a comfortable release and utilize it to expend the energy that comes with being angry.

As tough as anger is to express, often the feelings that lay beneath are more difficult to explore. Take the time to examine what you might be feeling beneath your anger. Can you find feelings of hurt, abandonment, disappointment, or sadness? Society sometimes stigmatizes these emotions as negative; if you express them, you may be considered weak and vulnerable. Recognition and exploration in this area will be meaningful as you strive toward anger management.

To help manage anger effectively, you may benefit from exploring how you handled anger in the past. Sometimes the tolerance for your mate's anger is a development of associations with the same types of behavior from your past. These associations with a former intimate relationship or from childhood experiences can impact your present ability to control anger. These earlier encounters helped shape your reactions and level of tolerance for the same behavior now exhibited by your mate. Simply put, your mate is "pushing the same buttons."

You will tolerate fewer of your mate's expressions of anger if they are the same behaviors you notice within yourself. The ability to find fault with your mate's conduct is easier and less challenging than to find fault within yourself. Your ability, though, to get in touch with your own anger is vital to your ability to better understand the survivor's anger. Without this understanding, you will continue to take personally the survivor's displaced anger for the perpetrator.

The following exercises will assist you in coming to terms with your anger. For more materials and exercises by other authors, see "Resources" under the heading "Books about Anger."

EXERCISE: ANGER #1

This first exercise will assist you in examining what your behaviors and reactions are to some of the hot points in your relationship. Once you identify these issues, you have taken the first step in beginning to change the behaviors and reactions which only seem to exacerbate both the survivor's anger and your own.

After you identify those behaviors, you will need to explore possible alternate responses to that potential hot point. The exercise is divided into three parts: A, B, and C.

Part A

List the things that the survivor does or says that you get angry at.

1._____

_____

2._____

_____

3._____

_____

4._____

_____

5._____

_____

EXERCISE: ANGER #1 (*continued*)

Part B

List what your reaction to each item in Part A is. Be sure to include your feelings, actions, statements, and behaviors.

1. _____

_____

_____

_____

2. _____

_____

_____

_____

3. _____

_____

_____

_____

4. _____

_____

_____

_____

5. _____

_____

_____

_____

EXERCISE: ANGER #1 (*continued*)

Part C

Finally, list some alternate ways to handle, act, or behave around the five things listed in Part A. For suggestions, refer to the recommendations listed earlier in this chapter.

1. _____

_____

_____

_____

2. _____

_____

_____

_____

3. _____

_____

_____

_____

4. _____

_____

_____

_____

5. _____

_____

_____

_____

WRITING EXERCISE: ANGER #2

This exercise will help you get in touch with how you have reacted to your own feelings of anger as a child. Do you deal with your own anger now in the same manner as when you were a child? Many adults find this to be the case.

Think back to when you were a child growing up in your home. Remember what it was like when you were angry as a child. Were you allowed to show your anger, or did you have to keep it inside? Did you yell and scream? Did you take your anger out on a sibling, a relative, a friend, or a pet? Did you ever take your anger out on yourself either verbally or physically? Take a moment now to write about an experience when you became angry as a child and how you reacted to it.

_____

_____

_____

_____

_____

_____

_____

_____

WRITING EXERCISE: ANGER #2 (*continued*)

_____

_____

_____

_____

_____

_____

_____

_____

_____

_____

_____

_____

_____

_____

EXERCISE: ANGER #3

Anger can entail a physical component as well as an emotional or psychological one. The following exercise will help you get in touch with how anger might be affecting you physically. If you can't get in touch now with what your physical reactions are, wait until the next time you get mad and take note of what is happening to you physically, e.g., you begin to sweat, your neck muscles get tense, you grind your teeth, your blood pressure rises, your heart beats faster, your breathing changes, or you get a pit in your stomach.

My physical reactions are:

_____

_____

_____

_____

_____

_____

_____

_____

_____

_____

WRITING EXERCISE: ANGER #4

This exercise will help you focus on your anger toward the perpetrator. As we discussed earlier in the workbook, you will go through your own process. Part of your process will involve grief and loss issues surrounding the changes in your relationship with the survivor. One of the feelings in this process is anger. You will find that much of this anger stems from your feelings toward the perpetrator of your mate's abuse.

If you don't find an appropriate way to express the anger you have at the perpetrator, you may find that you put yourself in a position similar to the survivor's. Namely, you will displace that anger onto another individual, most commonly your mate. The following exercise will assist you in constructively expressing that anger.

Like many of the other exercises in this workbook, this writing exercise is "freestyle," which means that for a specified period of time you will focus on the issue and feeling at hand, and then write about it. Don't be concerned about how much you write, and don't edit what you have written. The key is to just let your pen flow and put those thoughts and feelings down on paper. Take approximately ten to fifteen minutes to write about your feelings toward the perpetrator. Regardless of the number of perpetrators or whether you know their identities, try to get in touch with how these individuals have affected your and your mate's life. You may choose to include in this writing exercise any fantasy you have of what you would like to do to the perpetrator. Remember, this is just a writing exercise; your fantasy on paper is quite different from your decision to act it out in reality.

WRITING EXERCISE: ANGER #4 (*continued*)

_____

_____

_____

_____

_____

_____

_____

_____

_____

_____

_____

_____

_____

_____

_____

WRITING EXERCISE: ANGER #5

This exercise will help bring to your attention how some of the survivor's expressions of anger can trigger certain reactions in you. This triggering can be attributed to how you presently or previously expressed anger or how you identified an expression of anger in a family member such as a parent or sibling when you were growing up. To begin the exercise, first make a list of how your mate expresses anger.

My mate's anger:

_____

_____

_____

_____

_____

_____

_____

Next, make a list of the actions and behaviors you exhibit when you are angry.

My anger:

_____

_____

WRITING EXERCISE: ANGER #5 (*continued*)

My anger (*continued*):

_____

_____

_____

_____

_____

_____

Now make a list of those behaviors and expressions surrounding anger that you experienced from individuals in
your household when you were growing up.

Earlier anger:

_____

_____

_____

_____

_____

_____

_____

WRITING EXERCISE: ANGER #5 (*continued*)

Once you have completed all three lists, go back and find any similarities in them. Who are the similarities between: you and one of your parents, you and your mate, or your mate and one of your parents? Take the time to write about these similarities. How does it feel to experience these same behaviors surrounding anger? Do you have a particular reaction or fear? Follow the usual freestyle writing format.

_____

_____

_____

_____

_____

_____

_____

_____

_____

_____

_____

_____

Jack's Story

Anger at the perpetrator

With regard to the perpetrator, the macho side of me says I'd like to have him in the room alone, tied to a chair, and have a baseball bat. I'd love to really nail him! Not necessarily kill him but maiming him for life would be the best thing. I don't think he has any concept of what he has done to her, let alone us, or the families involved! I'd like to in some way let him know how many lives he has not ruined but had a major negative impact on. I understand a little bit more about the perpetrator and the type of person that does it, but if anything, I'd like to do more damage to him!

Concerning my anger, I think it wasn't until one group session when I just screamed and screamed again. I felt totally out of control, and it was a new feeling for me, and it really felt good. I think I've been very angry at the perpetrator, the court system, everyone involved with it, and the crap we've had to go through.

Bill's Story

Feelings toward the perpetrators

In regard to the perpetrators there has been a kind of evolution. There are times when I have felt great anger. I have ranted, raved, and been the champion of my wife's cause, almost ready to deal with those guys in a mortal manner. I wasn't in a position to do anything about it, so I just dealt with my feelings.

My wife and daughter were grateful that I was able to be angry at her perpetrators instead of being just another man she had to be careful of. I was someone she could trust. I was on her side. I guess as things have evolved and our relationship has become tighter, there isn't so much anger or blame directed at the perpetrators.

I don't blame anyone else for it, certainly not my wife. I think it's been more important to get our relationship together, stay focused, be honest with one another, and share our feelings. I think the perpetrator and his actions are less important now than thirty or thirty-five years ago. We cannot change that, but we can change the way we relate with one another. Both of us are focused on that now.

Sam's Story

Being a partner

The most difficult thing in being a partner, for me personally, is never knowing when the volcano is going to erupt, not knowing what's going to upset her. It isn't necessarily the same act on my part, the kids' part, or just the part of life. It depends on her; she's very moody. It probably depends on when she's having her flashbacks; you just never know. It feels like walking on eggshells!

Just feeling very tired and having to deal with it is very difficult for me when we are having one of these down periods. It's hard for me to want to be around; it's very draining. Even if we don't have a hassle, the thought that we may is enough to keep you on edge.

To me, that's the most difficult part: never really feeling comfortable in the relationship. Knowing there could be some anger expressed at almost anytime over almost anything. You never know when to expect it, or where it's going to come from. Most of the time I have no sense of comfort in being in my own house. It's not a place of sanctuary at all from work or whatever. It's a more threatening place than work. Really!

I guess I would say to any other partners out there, I think they have to be very, very emotionally strong. They have to realize that a lot of the anger that is expressed is not directed at them. Unfortunately, this isn't a short term experience in my opinion at all. It's very difficult over a long period of time to keep telling yourself over and over again, "I know it's not really me, it's the perpetrator."

After a while, it is a grinding down experience, and you have to be emotionally strong and dedicated to this person. Defer your own feelings and needs or else try and meet them in some other way than you are use to. You have to be really emotionally strong to focus on this. I wish anyone going through this a lot of luck.

Ten

Resources

This section lists various resources for partners, survivors, children, and families concerned about rape and childhood sexual abuse. The resources include publications as well as agency names and hotline phone numbers. Some of the resources listed may or may not be available in your area.

Books for Partners

Davis, L. (1991). *Allies in healing: When the person you love was sexually abused as a child.* New York: Harper Perennial.

Graber, K. (1991). *Ghosts in the bedroom: A guide for partners of incest survivors.* Deerfield Beach, Florida: Health Communications.

McEvoy, A. W., & Brookings, J. B. (1984). *If she is raped: A book for husbands, fathers, and male friends.* Holmes Beach, Florida: Learning Publications.

Spear, J. (1991). *How can I help her? A handbook for partners of women sexually abused as children.* Center City, Minnesota: Hazelden.

Books for Survivors
of Incest/Childhood Sexual Abuse

Bass, E., & Davis, L. (1988). *The courage to heal: A guide for women survivors of child sexual abuse.* New York: Harper & Row.

Bierker, S. (1989). *About sexual abuse.* Springfield, Illinois: Charles C. Thomas, Publisher.

Blume, E. S. (1990). *Secret survivors: Uncovering incest and its aftereffects in women.* New York: John Wiley & Sons.

Courtois, C. A. (1988). *Healing the incest wound: Adult survivors in therapy.* New York: W. M. Norton & Company.

Davis, L. (1991). *The courage to heal workbook: For women and men survivors of child sexual abuse.* New York: Harper & Row.

Kunzman, K. A. (1990). *The healing way: Adult recovery from childhood sexual abuse.* Center City, Minnesota: Hazelden.

Books for Survivors of Rape

Katz, J. H. (1984). *No fairy godmothers, no magic wands: The healing process after rape.* Saratoga, California: R & E Publishers.

Kelly, L. (1988). *Surviving sexual violence.* Minneapolis: University of Minnesota Press, 1988.

Madigan, L. (1991). *The second rape: Society's continued betrayal of the victim.* New York: Maxwell MacMillan.

Children's Books about Abuse

Adams, C., & Fay, J. (1981). *No more secrets: Protecting your child from sexual assault.* San Luis Obispo, California: Impact Publishers.

Freeman, L. (1983). *It's my body.* Seattle: Parenting Press, Inc.

Freeman, L. (1986). *Loving touches: A book for children about positive, caring kinds of touching.* Seattle: Parenting Press, Inc.

Girad, W. (1984). *My body is private.* Morton Grove, Illinois: Whitman & Company.

Jessie. (1991). *Please tell! A child's story about sexual abuse.* Center City, Minnesota: Hazelden, 1991.

Kehoe, P. (1987). *Something happened and I'm scared to tell.* Seattle: Parenting Press, Inc.

Books for Parents

Hart-Rossi, J. (1984). *Protect your child from sexual abuse: A parent's guide.* Seattle: Parenting Press, Inc.

Tschirhart-Sanford, L. (1980). *The silent children: A parent's guide to the prevention of child sexual abuse.* New York: McGraw-Hill Book Co.

Books about Anger

Lerner, H. G. (1985). *The dance of anger: A woman's guide to changing the patterns of intimate relationships.* New York: Harper & Row.

Weber, D. (1991). *Angry? Do you mind if I scream?* Deerfield Beach, Florida: Health Communications, Inc.

Weisinger, H. (1985). *Dr. Weisinger's anger workout book.* New York: Quill.

Books about Communication

Adler, R. B. (1977). *Confidence in communication: A guide to assertive and social skills.* New York: Holt, Rinehart and Winston.

Reardon, K. K. (1987). *Interpersonal communication: Where minds meet.* Belmont, California: Wadsworth.

Books about Grief and Loss

Orbuch, T. L. (Ed.). (1992). *Close relationship loss: Theoretical approaches.* New York: Springer-Verlag.

Tanner, I. S. (1976). *The gift of grief: Healing the pain of everyday losses.* New York: Hawthorn Books.

Books about Massage:

Lavabre, M. (1990). *Aromatherapy workbook.* Rochester, Vermont: Healing Arts Press.

Maxwell-Hudson, C. (1988). *The complete book of massage.* New York: Random House, Inc.

Montagu, A. (1986). *Touching.* New York: Harper & Row.

Tappan, F. M. (1988). *Healing massage techniques: Holistic, classic, and emerging methods.* 2nd ed. Norwalk, Connecticut: Appleton & Lange.

Hotline Numbers

California Youth Crisis: 1-800-448-4663
Center for Adults Abused Sexually As Children: 1-212-979-8613
Domestic Violence Hotline: 1-800-500-1119
Incest Helpline, New York: 1-212-227-3000
Incest Survivors Anonymous, California: 1-310-428-5599
Los Angeles County Rape & Battering Hotline: 1-310-392-8381
National Child Abuse Hotline: 1-800-422-4453
National Runaway Switchboard: 1-800-621-4000
National Victim Center, Virginia: 1-703-276-2880
Parents Anonymous: 1-909-621-6184
SIA (Survivors of Incest Anonymous)
    Baltimore, Maryland: 1-410-282-3400
    New York: 1-212-439-4778
    Sacramento, California: 1-916-537-7134
SNAP (Survivors Network Abused by Priests), Chicago:
    1-312-483-1059
The Valley Trauma Center (Northridge, California):
    1-818-886-0453

Support Organizations

Believe the Children. Provides educational information and support to professionals, parents, and concerned citizens regarding sexual and ritualistic exploitation of children. Chicago: 1-708-515-5432

Center for the Prevention of Sexual and Domestic Violence. Provides information to help communities respond to and prevent sexual and domestic violence. Washington: 1-206-634-1903

ChildHelp USA. Provides resources for adult survivors. National Child Abuse Hotline: 1-800-422-4453

Clearinghouse on Child Abuse and Neglect (CCAN), P.O. Box 1182, Washington, DC 20013: 1-703-385-7565

Coalition Against the Sexual Abuse of Young Children. Washington, DC: 1-202-966-7183

Echoes Network, Inc. Nationwide networking agency provides referrals for survivors if there is a local chapter. Portland: 1-503-281-8185

Incest Survivors Information Exchange. National newsletter publishes contributions (aricles, poetry, artwork) from men and women who have survived incest. P.O. Box 3399, New Haven, CT 06515

Incest Survivors Resource Network Internation. Resource for national organization welcomes calls from survivors of mother-son incest. New Mexico: 1-505-521-4260

Looking Up. Provides services to victims and survivors of incest. Augusta, Maine: 1-207-626-3402

Monarch Resources. Provides information on childhood sexual abuse and incest, ritual abuse, and partners and parents of survivors. Torrance, California: 1-310-373-1958

National Children's Advocacy Center. Provides treatment and intervention for sexually abused children and their families. Huntsville, Alabama: 1-205-533-5437

National Clearinghouse on Marital and Date Rape. Provides, through phone consultation, information and referral, reference, and research services on marital rape and acquaintance or date rape. Berkeley, California: 1-510-524-1582

Parents United/Daughters and Sons United. Assists sexually abused individuals. San Jose, California: 1-408-453-7611

SARA (Sexual Assault Recovery Anonymous) Society. British Columbia, Canada: 1-604-584-2626

VOICES in Action. Organization for survivors and partners. Chicago: 1-312-327-1500

Bibliography

Blume, E. S. (1990). *Secret survivors: Uncovering incest and its aftereffects in women.* New York: John Wiley & Sons.

Burgess, A. W. (1985). *Rape and sexual assault.* New York: Garland Publishing.

Calhoun, K. S., & Atkeson, B. M. (1991). *Treatment of rape victims: Facilitating psychosocial adjustment.* New York: Pergamon Press.

Clark, R. E., & Clark, J. F. (1989). *The Encyclopedia of Child Abuse.* New York: Facts on File, Inc.

Cohen, L. J. (1988). Providing treatment and support for partners of sexual assault survivors. *Psychotherapy, 25,* 94-8.

Courtois, C. A. (1988). *Healing the incest wound: Adult survivors in therapy.* New York: W. W. Norton & Company.

Davis, L. (1991). *Allies in healing: When the person you love was sexually abused as a child.* New York: Harper Perennial.

Federal Bureau of Investigation. (1993). *Crime in the United States 1993.* Washington, DC: U.S. Government Printing Office.

Graber, K. (1991). *Ghosts in the bedroom: A guide for partners of incest survivors.* Deerfield Beach, Florida: Health Communications.

Grauerholz, E., & Koralewski, M. A. (1991). Sexual coercion: A sourcebook on its nature, causes, and prevention. In E. Grauerholz & M. A. Koralewski (Eds.), *Rape* (3-15). Lexington, Massachusetts: Lexington Books.

Halpern, S. (1978). *Rape: Helping the victim.* Oradell, New Jersey: Medical Economics Company.

Holstrom, L. L., & Burgess, M. A. (1979). Rape: The husband's and boyfriend's initial reactions. *The Family Coordinator, 28,* 321-30.

Jackson, J. L., et al. (1990). Young adult women who report childhood intrafamilial sexual abuse: Subsequent adjustment. *Archives of Sexual Behavior, 19,* 211-21.

Johnson, S. M. (1989). Integrating marital and individual therapy for incest survivors: A case study. *Psychotherapy, 26,* 96-103.

Kelly, L. (1988). *It leaves a mark: Coping with the consequences of sexual violence.* Minneapolis: University of Minnesota Press.

Ledray, L. E. (1990). Counseling rape victims: The nursing challenge. *Perspectives in Psychiatric Care, 26,* 21-7.

Lerner, H. G. (1985). *The dance of anger: A woman's guide to changing the patterns of intimate relationships.* New York: Harper & Row.

Lindberg, F. H., & Distad, L. D. (1985). Survival responses to incest: Adolescents in crisis. *Child Abuse & Neglect, 9,* 521-6.

Maltz, W. (1988). Identifying and treating the sexual repercussions of incest: A couples therapy approach. *Journal of Sex & Marital Therapy, 14,* 142-70.

McCahill, T. W., Meyer, L. C., & Fischman, A. M. (1979). *The aftermath of rape.* Lexington, Massachusetts: Lexington Books.

McCombie, S. L. (1980). The rape crisis intervention handbook. In S. L. McCombie (Ed.), *Counseling the mates and families of rape victims* (173-81). New York: Plenum Press.

McEvoy, A. W., & Brookings, J. B. (1984). *If she is raped: A book for husbands, fathers, and male friends.* Holmes Beach, Florida: Learning Publications.

Miller, W. R., Williams, A. M., & Bernstein, M. H. (1982). The effects of rape on marital and sexual adjustment. *The American Journal of Family Therapy, 10,* 51-8.

Mio, J. S., & Foster, J. D. (1991). The effects of rape upon victims and families: Implications for a comprehensive family therapy. *The American Journal of Family Therapy, 19,* 147-59.

Quina, K., & Carlson, N. L. (1989). *Rape, incest, and sexual harassment: A guide for helping survivors.* New York: Praeger.

Rodkin, L. I., Hunt, E. J., & Cowan, S. D. A men's support group for significant others of rape victims. *Journal of Marital and Family Therapy, 8,* 91-7.

Schmittroth, Linda (Ed.). (1991). *Statistical record of women worldwide.* Detroit: Gale Research Inc.

Stuart, I. R., & Greer, J. G. (1984). Victims of sexual aggression: Treatment of children, women, and men. In I. R. Stuart & J. G. Greer (Eds.), *Marital and sexual dysfunction following rape: Identification and treatment* (197-210). New York: Van Nostrand Reinhold Company.

Trepper, T. S., & Barrett, M. J. (1983). *Systemic treatment of incest.* New York: Brunner/Mazel.

Walker, L. E. (1988). *Handbook on sexual abuse of children: Assessment and treatment issues.* New York: Springer.

Warner, C. G. (1980). *Rape and sexual assault: Management & intervention.* Germantown, Maryland: Aspen.

Weber, D. (1991). *Angry? Do you mind if I scream?* Deerfield Beach, Florida: Health Communications, Inc.

Weisinger, H. (1985). *Dr. Weisinger's workout book.* New York: Quill.

Books about Grieving and Loss

HEALING OUR LOSSES: A Journal for Working through Your Grief

Jack Miller, PhD

Paper, $10.95, 104 pages, 7" X 10"
ISBN 0-89390-255-1

In *Healing Our Losses*, the author shares experiences of loss in his own life and guides you to record your memories, thoughts, and feelings about loss in your life. Ample journaling space is provided. Working through this book can comfort anyone who has suffered the loss of a loved one and can help eventually heal the pain. Journaling may be done alone by an individual or in a group setting.

MORGAN'S BABY SISTER: A Read-Aloud Book for Families Who Have Experienced the Death of a Newborn

Patricia Polin Johnson & Donna Reilly Williams

Paper, $11.95, 64 pages, 6" x 9"
ISBN 0-89390-257-8

A read-aloud story of a little girl, Morgan, and her parents, who try to sort out their feelings of confusion and grief after the death of their premature baby. This can assist parents and adult caregivers with the difficult and often painful task of helping children understand their feelings about tragedies they experience.

Order from your local bookseller, or use the order form on the last page.

Books for Inspiration and Growth

RISING ABOVE:
A Guide
to Overcoming Obstacles
and Finding Happiness

Jerry Wilde, PhD

Paper, $14.95, 144 pages, 5½" x 8½"
ISBN 0- 89390-345-0

Everyone experiences some setbacks, losses, or health problems. Such events can permanently change a person's life for the worse—or they can be opportunities for growth. Pain can be a good friend asking you to change. This book, by a psychologist who had to face his own life-threatening disease, lays out some tools that will help you face any dilemma with a minimum of suffering. Great referral book for counselors.

> "This book is a wonderful guide for living a simpler, less frustrating and more responsible life. Dr. Wilde's use of these ideas and techniques in his own life, along with his courage and determination, will be an inspiration to every reader."
> — Sandy Tellefson, MSSW

WRITING YOUR WAY
TO WHOLENESS:
Creative Exercises
for Personal Growth

Terre Ouwehand

Paper, $17.95, 220 pages, 6" x 9"
ISBN 0-89390-312-4

Are you trying to grow spiritually? If you are a budding writer—or you just enjoy journalizing or scribbling on napkins—here's good news. Terre Ouwehand, a creative writing instructor, uncovers the link between your most casual writing and your spiritual growth. Try her tips on freewriting, list-making, clustering, and streamwriting. Select from hundreds of exercises to uncover your creativity and discover your real feelings. Writing and soulwork has never been so much fun.

Order from your local bookseller, or use the order form on the last page.

Books for Developing Coping Skills

SO, WHAT IS ASSERTIVENESS?
An Assertiveness Training Course

Chrissie Whitehead

Paper, $29.95, 72 pages,
perforated, 8½" x 11",
ISBN 0-89390-296-9
North American Rights

This material contains exercises to help
identify assertive, aggressive, and
passive behaviors while applying this
knowledge to everyday life. Includes
photocopiable handouts. May be used
in high school or adult education
groups.

FACING VIOLENCE:
Discussion-Starting Skits
for Teenagers

R. William Pike

Paper $19.95, 192 pages, 6" x 9"
ISBN 0-89390-344-2

You can get teens to talk about their
problems by using simple dramas.
Facing Violence provides you with 40
skits addressing violence in schools,
violence in the home, violent
language, violence and dating,
violence in society, and solutions to
violence. These skits require no
rehearsal and can be performed on
the spot in a classroom setting. Try
them. They work!

> "This book is a hands-on resource
> useful for anyone who wants to
> help kids improve their lives. The
> situations are straight-forward,
> thought-provoking and deal with
> issues that are a part of
> adolescent life in every school
> and every setting." — Susan
> Finkelstein, MD, Director of
> Adolescent Services, Silver Hill
> Hospital, New Canaan, CT

Order from your local bookseller, or use the order form on the last page.

Tools for Living

PARTNERS IN HEALING: Redistributing Power in the Counselor-Client Relationship

Barbara Friedman, PhD

Paper, $14.95, 144 pages, 5½" x 8½"
ISBN 0-89390-226-8

Dr. Barbara Friedman proposes a therapeutic model in which counselor and client interact as equal partners in the healing process. This book is must reading for therapists, counselors, and clients.

HOW TO NETWORK AND SELECT A MENTOR

Paul Stevens

Paper, $8.95, 96 pages, 4¼" x 7"
ISBN 0-89390-346-9
North American Rights

As you discover networking, you will be amazed at how helpful and supportive others can be—even people you don't know well. Strategies that worked well for them could be useful to you, not just in your work life but in any aspect of your life. But you won't learn about those strategies unless you talk to other people. In this book an internationally recognized expert shows you how.

MEN ARE NO DAMN GOOD (PENDING FURTHER RESEARCH): Essays on Becoming a Man

Eugene J. Webb,

Illustrated by C. P. Houston

Paper, $14.95, 192 pages, 5½" x 8½"
ISBN 0- 89390-343-4

Here's a book that unlocks one of the secrets of the universe: What is it with men anyway? But be warned, this is not a self-help book. "We men don't need help," says author Eugene Webb. "And you gals know by now that you're wasting your time slipping this or any book under our coffee cups or stuck behind our toothbrushes. We know what you're doing. It won't work." What guys need is to laugh at themselves, brag about themselves, and cry about themselves—and have a good time doing it. So these witty essays about becoming a man are just a pleasure. Any helpful insights and unnerving pieces of wisdom are totally accidental.

Order from your local bookseller, or use the order form on the last page.

Books for Working Through a Crisis

WHEN YOUR LONG-TERM MARRIAGE ENDS:
A Workbook for Divorced Women

Elaine Newell

Paper, $14.95, 144 pages, 6" x 9",
ISBN 0-89390-291-8

When Your Long-Term Marriage Ends is a workbook written especially for the woman who finds herself facing the challenging transition of a divorce. This book leads the reader through the stages of panic, rejection, anger, loneliness, awareness, responsibility, and, finally, forgiveness.

THE CURE:
The Hero's Journey with Cancer

G. Frank Lawlis, PhD

Paper, $9.95, 64 pages, 5½" x 8½"
ISBN 0-89390-273-X

$39.95 Caregiver's Kit
(book, two audiocassettes, caregiver's guide)

This fable—about a wolf who consults other animals for a cure for a mysterious disease—is designed to help people with cancer confront their fears. Give this book to adult cancer patients or adapt it for oral storytelling to children and adults.

Order Form

Order these resources from your local bookstore, or mail this form to:

QTY	TITLE	PRICE	TOTAL

Subtotal: _____

CA residents add 7¼% sales tax
(Santa Clara Co. residents, 7¾%): _____

Postage and handling
($3 for order up to $30; 10% of order
over $30 but less than $150;
$15 for order of $150 or more): _____

Total: _____

Resource Publications, Inc.
160 E. Virginia Street #290 - MK
San Jose, CA 95112-5876
(408) 286-8505
(408) 287-8748 FAX

☐ My check or money order is enclosed.

☐ Charge my ☐ VISA ☐ MC.

Expiration Date _____

Card # _____ - _____ - _____ - _____

Signature _____

Name (print) _____

Institution _____

Street _____

City/State/ZIP _____